Leaving The Reason Torn

Commendations for *Leaving The Reason Torn:*

"This timely book provides not only an inspiring introduction to R. S. Thomas' theology of the cross and resurrection but a clarion call to a different way of doing theology: one that lives with loose ends, ragged edges and suggestion rather than clear answers and certainty. It is worth reading not only for what it says but how it says it."
Paula Gooder lectures and writes on biblical studies and is Canon Theologian of Birmingham and Guildford Cathedrals.

"Theologians often want to confine God to the limits of their own pet theories. Poets – and supremely R. S. Thomas – offer us a sense of God less easy to tame, released from the straightjacket of academic discipline. Alison Goodlad brings this contrast into clear view and convincingly shows the disrupting wisdom of the poet. This is a fascinating and important book."
Giles Fraser is a former Canon Chancellor of St Paul's Cathedral.

"R. S. Thomas is one of the truly great voices of twentieth century verse, and a man whose startlingly honest wrestling with faith, as with Welsh identity, continues to resonate in the new millennium. This book does a great service in revisiting his work and showing how it illuminates core Christian convictions in a sceptical age."
Aled Edwards is chief executive of Cytûn: Churches Together in Wales.

Comments on earlier work by Alison Goodlad on R. S. Thomas:

"The new is never without scars from the old, so that we are always left with what is ambiguous and somewhat unresolved. Poetry is the right medium for the 'counter testimony' of the Gospel, and Alison Goodlad has shown that in R. S. Thomas with great precision. Her study is most suggestive."
Walter Brueggemann is a leading biblical scholar, and the former William Marcellus McPheeters Professor of Old Testament at Columbia Theological Seminary, USA.

"A really good and interesting piece. [...] I think that poetry is precisely the vehicle which allows people to 'inhabit' more than one register or orientation: because it deals in resonance and metaphor, it is always double or treble vision."
Rowan Williams, Archbishop of Canterbury.

Leaving The Reason Torn
Re-thinking cross and resurrection through R. S. Thomas

Alison Goodlad

with a Foreword by

Professor Lord Harries of Pentregarth

Shoving Leopard

First published in 2012 by

Shoving Leopard
Flat 2F3, 8 Edina Street
Edinburgh
EH7 5PN
United Kingdom
http://www.shovingleopard.com/

Cover: Nial Smith Design, 13/4 Annandale Street, Edinburgh, EH7 4AW

ISBN 978-1-905565-18-4

A catalogue record for this book is available from the British Library.

Contents

Acknowledgements

I am particularly grateful to Christopher Southgate, University of Exeter, who encouraged, guided and supported me during the writing of this book and to Tony Brown, University of Bangor, who generously gave of his time in reading through the manuscript. Their advice and corrections have been invaluable but all remaining errors/ misunderstandings are of course my own.

Richard Skinner first alerted me to the poetry of R. S. Thomas and I am so grateful for that introduction. I would also like to thank David Catchpole whose inspiring scholarship and personal warmth has spurred me on to keep asking the questions and seeking for answers.

I would like to thank Janet de Vigne of Shoving Leopard for being enthusiastic about publishing the book and Simon Barrow for his editorship and long-term support. Thanks also to Nial Smith for his creative cover.

Gwydion (R. S. Thomas's son) and Kunjana Thomas have been very supportive and I am grateful to them for kindly granting permission to quote from R. S. Thomas's poetry 1955-1988. I am equally grateful to Bloodaxe Books for permission to quote from R. S. Thomas Collected Later Poems 1988-2000 (Bloodaxe Books, 2004).

I am grateful to Baron Harries of Pentregarth for kindly agreeing to write a foreword to this book, and to others who have offered commendations.

Closer to home, I am only beginning to appreciate the extent to which my Father, Ron Coleman, has sown the seeds in me of a desire for theological exploration. I am deeply grateful too for the constant interest and support of my Mother, Peggy Coleman (who died in March 2010) who was always asking me how I was getting on with my book. But it is my husband Chris who bears the brunt of my preoccupation with R. S. Thomas and he has been a patient and attentive listener as I try out on him my latest thoughts, and it is to him that I dedicate this book with gratitude and love.

Foreword

The poetry of R. S. Thomas both disturbs and keeps open the possibility of Christian faith: and the two are integrally linked. It disturbs because it often puts into words feelings which most religious believers would find impossible to utter; yet this carries with it the presumption and possibility of faith.

This book by Alison Goodlad is a particular help in understanding the relationship of this poetry to faith, first of all because it sets the poetry against a wider background. In the earlier chapters of the book she shows the limitations of traditional ways of trying to understand the universal significance of Christ's death and resurrection, the nature of religious language, and how we can best understand the Old and New Testaments. Then she considers the implications of this in relation to the theme of cross and resurrection in the poetry, drawing on much that is less familiar as well as some well-loved poems.

Iris Murdoch once wrote, "All that consoles is fake". It is a sentence that states in lapidary form our deep suspicion of anything that smacks of a happy resolution tacked on at the end. Thomas was deeply aware of how profoundly this attitude of Murdoch had sunk into 20th century consciousness, at once soaked in Freud and acutely aware of the terrible suffering of that century.

There is no easy consolation in R. S. Thomas. Yet does not the Christian faith proclaim resurrection and the final triumph of a Divine loving purpose? Thomas has been criticised for focussing on the cross and saying too little about the resurrection and nothing about the Holy Spirit. One of the important features of this book by Alison Goodlad is the way she shows that it is not just the cross but the resurrection which runs through so much of the poetry, and how integrally linked they are.

In fact this is much closer to how the early Christians saw the matter than the later mediaeval period when cross and resurrection are sharply separated. In the passion sarcophagus of the 4th century one of the striking features is the way that the cross and resurrection of Christ is seen as one unified saving event, and the same is true in the 6th century Rabbula Gospels. In Thomas' poems the resurrection is certainly not a happy ending tacked on, or indeed any kind of reversal but a revelation of the meaning and ultimate vindication of Divine love on the cross.

R. S. Thomas had a sceptical mind, of the most dangerous sort: a moral scepticism about the goodness of the creator. Yet behind his austere persona are intense feelings, not just of sensitivity to human suffering, but also of a fiercely searching, faithful Christian faith. Another feature of this book is the way Alison Goodlad shows the continuing tension in Thomas between his intellect and those feelings. A line of Samuel Beckett comes to mind: "A heart in my head" – though that perhaps implies a greater degree of synthesis than is apparent in the poetry of Thomas. It is the nature of tension to be unresolved.

All who respond to the poetry of R. S. Thomas, but especially those who are uneasy and unsatisfied by traditional Christian understandings of Christ's cross and resurrection, will find much helpful illumination in this thorough but readable study.

Professor Lord Harries of Pentregarth
Easter 2012

Introduction

Christians agree that the death and resurrection of Jesus is central to their faith. But as soon as we try to understand the 'how' and 'why', it becomes much more difficult to articulate this belief. The early Christians grappled with this too and used a variety of imagery to express their experience. It is important to realize that the experience came first and the explanations came later. But if the experience is to be shared, communication is vital and words form an important part of this. Language is the key.

Poets are the supreme magicians with language, being able to conjure such breadth, depth and height from the same words as are used mundanely by the rest of us. We need the prosaic of course. But in our necessary struggles to understand, and particularly to appropriate that central tenet of the Christian faith – the death and resurrection of Christ – we may have tried too neatly to encapsulate in theory what is in fact far more mysterious and challenging than such theories appear to allow.

Formal explanations of the crucifixion and resurrection are known as atonement theories. The early Christians, whose witness we have in the Bible, were certainly looking for ways to understand and communicate the events that had taken place; events which had overturned their world. But the language they used was metaphorical. Over the years, the process of trying to express the meaning of the crucifixion and resurrection continued, and in different cultural contexts new theories emerged building on the language from the Bible, but seeking to be more rational and less suggestive.

This book is not intended to say that such enterprises have been wrong or that they do not have their place. But some of us have found the theoretical approach to be insufficient. We need creative minds, including the poets, to help us grapple with the Easter events and to enter into this world with mind and heart.

The 20th century Welsh poet/priest R. S. Thomas is such a creative mind. His language is profoundly unsettling at times, courageously saying what some may think but feel unable to utter. He looks at things from more than one perspective, trying out one idea before moving on to another way of seeing. His poetry is personal in the sense that it is his own faith journey he is expressing: a continual wrestling with the God to whom he is totally committed but whom he struggles to understand in the light of a suffering but dazzlingly beautiful world.

Crucifixion and resurrection language permeates Thomas's poetry and allows us to appreciate that crucifixion and resurrection is a way of being in this world; that Good Friday and Easter Sunday encapsulate a recurring dynamic.

In the first chapter I give an overview of the main atonement theories and show why it is that these can only take us so far in engaging with the death and resurrection of Christ. Others have also found that the rich metaphors of the Bible have been somewhat tamed by the more rational analytical approach and want to open the doors to a less constricted approach. It seems that the explanatory approaches that may have served people well in other times are not so appropriate in our current Western cultural climate, in our time which goes under the slippery and rather ill-defined term, post-modernity. We need the different voice of the creative artist to help us.

But what is the nature of poetry, how do we define it, and why is it so helpful for the investigation and appropriation of religious truth? I look at this in the second chapter and explore the use of metaphor, particularly in relation to crucifixion and resurrection. Perhaps poetry also enables us to hold together opposites, without the one dissolving into the other, and the poet William Blake's concept of 'contraries' is enlightening in this regard.

The next two chapters aim to set R. S. Thomas's poetry within a biblical framework. Thomas fed on the Bible as well as being alive to the world about him: the biblical text lived in him and resonated with his being. He was certainly discriminating in his appreciation of the Bible. Not all texts had the same value for him. But he found rich resources there that supported his questioning and subversive, yet ultimately affirming, approach.

So in chapter three, I look at the Old Testament background that will be especially helpful in our reading of R. S. Thomas. The Old Testament scholar Walter Brueggemann is perhaps one of the foremost voices of our day to have drawn attention to the untamed nature of the biblical text, and the God to whom it witnesses. His literary approach has much in common with the spirit of the poet Thomas. Brueggemann has also shown us how, in the Psalms particularly, but repeated in other texts, there is a dynamic present that moves from orientation, though disorientation, towards new orientation. This is an echo in the Old Testament of the crucifixion and resurrection in the New Testament.

Those biblical writers who speak of the descent into disorientation, who challenge the received wisdom of the day, Brueggemann calls the voices of counter-testimony in the trial to establish what is true. It seems that the mantle of counter-testimony in the pursuit of truth has fallen in our times on the poet R. S. Thomas. His voice has taken up those raised in the Psalms and in Job for example, two biblical books that we know Thomas deeply appreciated, and he gives Christian expression to the ancient dilemmas. The voice of R. S. Thomas is one that is rare in Christianity, but typical in the Jewish faith, of challenging and arguing with God.

But has not the story of the New Testament resolved the perplexities of the Old Testament? In chapter four I suggest that, in our desire to defend God, we have lost sight of the scandal of the cross. Scholarly study of the historical Jesus has shown that, in contrast to the atonement theories that make the cross seem inevitable and part of the plan from the beginning, the evidence from the historical/critical investigation of Jesus does not point that way. The problem of innocent suffering in this world, the subject that fascinates and torments R. S. Thomas, is as acute as ever in the crucifixion of Jesus. The dynamic of orientation, disorientation and new orientation is present in the New Testament and continues to find expression in our world.

This rhythm is found too in the poetry of R. S. Thomas in which he engages with crucifixion and resurrection. By putting Thomas's poetry within this loose framework, is this simply the substitution of one theory for other discarded ones? To some extent it is, of course, a theory. But primarily it is more in the nature of an observation than an explanation. This is how things are in God's world, but leaves open the challenges, the protest and the mystery and does not finally require that all is neatly resolved.

Having looked at why atonement theory on its own is insufficient to help us engage with the crucifixion and resurrection and considered the possibilities that poetry opens up; seen how deeply embedded R. S. Thomas is in the biblical way of seeing the world, as witnessed to in both the Old and New Testaments; we then turn to the poetry of R. S. Thomas.

A feature of Thomas's poetry is that one poem never says it all and you need to read one poem against another. The same themes and language recur across the years, but different insights, different perspectives emerge. It is helpful therefore to read Thomas's poetry in chronological order, so that these similarities and differences can gradually emerge.

The next four chapters explore the poetry of R. S. Thomas as it unfolds over the course of his long and productive poetic career. Chapter five concentrates on his earlier years, when he was shocked into poetry by wrestling with the struggles and the suffering he observed amongst his rural Welsh parishioners. The Welsh landscape is very predominant in this poetry.

As he grew older the focus shifted to a more explicit concentration on religious themes and he became courageously experimental in his poetry, the subject of chapter six. Chapter seven concerns the destinations he had in view, and the journey he travelled. As he approaches the end of his life we will look, in chapter eight, at the extent to which he continued to be that voice of counter-testimony, with no diminution of his poetic abilities. He never called a truce with the furies!

In the Afterword I will review what I believe to be the impact Thomas has made on our engagement with crucifixion and resurrection and why he seems to be particularly helpful for our time. There are many people who find in him a voice which articulates what they have felt but cannot say. But his very relevance for our day is not because he speaks a new gospel but because his is the voice for us of counter-testimony in the search for truth, a voice that speaks for and to those who wish to engage seriously with the perplexities of life in the light of God and the biblical witness.

And can poetry, Thomas's poetry, make us to be different people, for atonement is not intended to be simply an intellectual exercise but a way of changing, of being made new? This is where the strength of poetry is evident, for it challenges the whole person, not just the mind but the heart also. To give ourselves seriously to the poetry demands a great deal but our mistake is to think perhaps that religion is easy, demands little. R. S. Thomas was under no such illusion and his life of prayer and exploration witnesses to that. He has given us the poetry born out of such a life and this enables us in turn to confront the mind-numbing, tearing perplexities of life, the crucifying issues, but it also allows the spirit to soar in the hope of resurrection. As the words continue to reverberate in our hearts and minds, we can go on being changed.

Reason may be torn, but the way is left open to the torn God, for us to experience at-one-ment.

Chapter One
Theory is not enough

Atonement is a somewhat confusing term because it is not always used in the same way. Literally it is 'at-one-ment' and speaks of a bringing together, a reconciliation, of two parties. But the word has somewhat shifted from this definition and is often understood to mean an *act* of atonement, where something is done or said in order to make good in some way for a wrong.

In the novel *The Kite Runner* (Hosseini, 2003: 1,2) Amir, now living in the US but originally from Afghanistan, opens his story with a phone call from his relative, Rahim Khan in Pakistan, inviting Amir to come and see him. Something very bad happened in Amir's life when he was twelve for which he felt culpable; events had taken place the memory of which he had tried to bury but in fact haunted him. 'Standing in the kitchen with the receiver to my ear, I knew it wasn't Rahim Khan on the line. It was my past of unatoned sins.' But Rahim Khan had left him with the words '*There is a way to be good again*' (emphasis in the original). There was something he could do which would not remove his previous sins, but allow him to make atonement, and thus learn how to be good again, give him a future where the past no longer bedevilled him.

So there is the suggestion that atonement is not only about the reconciliation, but also about how it is achieved. Christians believe that the death and resurrection of Christ was in some way instrumental in bringing peace, reconciliation, and atonement, and in showing a way to be good again. But how? Atonement theories are the way in which an explanation is offered for that 'how' and to provide a bridge from the Easter event in the past to present experience.

Trying to find words to give shape and meaning to what had happened in the crucifixion and resurrection is a task that goes back to the first witnesses of the event. They started with an experience that they sought to understand and communicate using a variety of imagery drawn from their own world. These early metaphors have, over the succeeding centuries, formed the basis of explanatory atonement theories. There are no hard and fast rules as to what each separate theory comprises and language from one is often used in another approach.

My intention here is not to fully explore all possible defects in atonement theory, but to draw attention to the problems arising from treating the biblical imagery as literal explanation. Neither is it my intention to say that atonement theory does not have its place, for we are meaning seeking creatures and theoretical explanation forms part of this. But in this sphere there is a point at which explanation runs into the ground and we need the complementary voices of the storyteller, the artist and the poet in order to explore more fully crucifixion and resurrection.

In the description below of the various atonement theories, I am utilizing the frameworks of legality, sacrifice, victory and example. I am following here the groupings given by Paul Fiddes in his helpful and clearly written book *Past Event and Present Salvation* (1989).

The legal theory has at its core the demands of justice but the movement from the Hebrew law court imagery to a legal theory is perhaps one of the most contentious areas of atonement theory. As Fiddes says, 'Somehow, because Jesus Christ was condemned as a criminal in a human law court, we have been declared to be innocent in God's sight. But in that 'somehow' there is vast room not only for mystery but also for misunderstanding' (1989: 83). The law court imagery, married with other ideas, came to be transformed in other times and places until it became what is now known as the penal substitution theory. This is the view that Christ's death is deemed to be a substitutionary one in which he took the punishment which, in legal terms, was required of humanity. Without this death, God's righteous demands could not be met and a pardon could not be issued. In some Christian circles this is *the* understanding of the work of Christ, to the exclusion of all other approaches.

This theory is subject to a variety of criticisms. For example, it makes God subject to the law. It exalts law whereas Christ suffered an innocent death condemned by the law. The death of someone other than the guilty one is seen as meeting the demands of justice. It ignores the reality of forgiveness in the Old Testament. There is also the impersonal quality of a pardon; and lastly, it implies that divine sanction is given to violent death. So the penal substitution theory is problematic for these reasons, but the main point I wish to make here is that this theory proposes that the death of Christ makes logical, rational sense. It becomes a mechanical process. In this way, it does not face certain issues raised by the gospel story (which we will be exploring in more detail in chapter four), whereby God appears to be powerless in the face of evil.

Secondarily, Christ's death can be viewed in terms of sacrifice. Sacrifice was part of the ancient world and belonged in a cultic setting. In the Temple worship, sacrifice played an intrinsic part and could be an expression of thanksgiving, praise, gift and repentance. But it was in particular the offering for sin that the early Christians saw as illuminating the death of Christ. Sacrifice was not seen in the Old Testament as a substitute for repentance, it was an expression, a costly one, of that attitude: it was the way the ancient Hebrews experienced restoration of fellowship with God. It was natural therefore, in looking for imagery to express their sense of being at one with God through Christ, for the early Christians to use the language of sacrifice.

But the conceptual framework followed the experience. As Fiddes says 'The experience of forgiveness and reconciliation came first, and then they interpreted it by saying 'It's like a sacrifice' and 'yet it's for all time' (1989: 68). Fiddes also points out that 'The Old Testament offers no proper theory as to *how* the act of sacrifice could remove sin and guilt from the community or from individuals within it' (1989: 68). So the early Christians were not transposing a theoretical explanation from one context to another, they were giving expression, in imagery familiar to their world, of a new experience in Christ. It seems appropriate, therefore, that we should treat the language of sacrifice at a different level to that of explanation, and it is here that the creative artist may be able to help.

Turning now to a third atonement theory that sees Christ's death and resurrection in terms of victory, it is evident, even in our own time, that there appear to be destructive powers which seem to run deeper than the sum total of individual actions. But for the early Christians, the apprehension of such danger was even more pronounced, and lives were lived under the ever present and serious threat of demonic powers. Therefore, to describe Christ's death in terms of a defeat of evil (although extraordinarily this was through weakness and not through strength) is to tell of a liberating gospel. There is no question that this has a powerful effect imaginatively, but if it is again regarded as an *explanation* we are immediately faced with the problem Fiddes poses: 'In what sense *could* evil have been defeated in the cross of Jesus, if its power seems undiminished today?' (1989: 113). As an explanatory theory appealing to reason, this question seems unanswerable. So again we see that atonement theories can only carry us so far in probing the meaning of the death of Christ.

The fourth theoretical framework understands the effectiveness of Christ's death to lie in its power as an example. As one who has shown what it is to live, and to die, an authentic human life, the power of Jesus' example is irrefutable. But this again poses questions as to what sort of world this is when a good man can die in shame and agony, and it is this last area to which the poetry of R. S. Thomas speaks most powerfully – for he opens up an exploration of why it seems that the negative is as much part of God's world as the positive. A theory which says that Christ died as an example provokes as many questions as it answers, and the voice of the poet is invaluable in exploring this further.

At the commencement of his book on atonement theories, Fiddes quotes, as a cautionary tale, from C. S. Lewis, who had long puzzled over the 'how' of the atonement and had come to the conclusion that 'a man can accept what Christ has done without knowing how it works' and that 'the thing itself is infinitely more important than any explanations the theologians have produced' (1989: 4). At the conclusion of that same book, Fiddes says: 'If God did indeed expose his being to death on the cross, as the doctrine of atonement affirms, then he himself encountered what was strange; this too is part of the reason why those who share his cross enter a kingdom which cannot be mapped by human explanations. The creative power of the cross heals our relationships, but also plunges us into the Golgotha of the Spirit (Hegel's phrase). Or, as Bonhoeffer says daringly, "Christians stand by God in the hour of his grieving" ' (1989: 218,219). Atonement theories, explanations, can only take us so far into this mystery. If, unlike Fiddes, people do not recognize them as partial avenues only, then it is possible to protect ourselves from the offence, the scandal, of the cross.

Other voices have also been raised in recent years protesting against the theoretical approach to the death and resurrection and saying that this has moved us some distance from the way the issue was approached in the New Testament. John Driver, in *Understanding the Atonement for the Mission of the Church* explores this area. He says that '[r]ather than logical, rationally satisfying definitions of the meaning of the work of Christ, we are confronted in the New Testament with a variety of images' (2005: 244). He goes on to say, 'However, we do well to resist pressure to systematize the manifold imagery of the New Testament. A pluralism of images is essential for communicating the meaning of the work of Christ in its fullness' (2005: 247).

The pluralism found in the New Testament perhaps strikes a chord in us two thousand years later, for post-modernity, with its plurality of interpretative lenses, is content to allow multiple images to exist side by side, and not to require a decision over which is the most satisfactory. A theoretical approach resonates more closely with the spirit of modernity, where reason is preeminent. Images can coexist, but theories tend to exclude other points of view. 'A theory includes an intentional concern for consistency and logic with a view to being able to protect itself from other less adequate formulations', says Driver (2005: 37).

A theory also gives the feeling that somehow everything is under control. But this was not how it seemed for the early witnesses to the Easter events. 'For the early disciples, the cross was a puzzle to be contemplated, a paradox to be explained, a question on which to reflect' (Green & Baker, 2000: 16). As the title of their book suggests, *Recovering the Scandal of the Cross: Atonement in New Testament and Contemporary Contexts,* Green and Baker seek to show that the meaning of the death and resurrection of Christ is not a self-evident truth, and we need to bring to it all the resources of imagination and language, and even then we will not have done enough. They say: 'We have come to the conclusion that this question is incapable of being addressed fully or decisively for all times and places. This is because of the limitations of human language, and of even our most impressive metaphors, to account fully for this mystery, the cross of Christ' (2000: 200).

James Alison, in *On Being Liked,* is an additional voice protesting that the very need for theory is the problem. He says: 'The first point I'd like to make is that a central problem with atonement theory, regardless of its content, is that it is a theory. By this I mean that, merely setting out an explanation, of 'how Christ saved us' in a tidy story such as the one we are accustomed to, runs the grave danger …. of being hijacked by a modern need for theory. What a friend of mine called 'physics envy'. . .The need is linked to the Cartesian world of clear and distinct ideas, based on mathematics being somehow the truest form of truth; anything more narrative, being more bodily and thus more subject to the slings and arrows of outrageous fortune, is somehow unsatisfactory and prone to being an inferior mode of truth-telling' (2003: 20).

So again we see that, in the pursuit of truth, there is not just one avenue. Modernity favoured the neat and tidy explanations, whereas post-modernity is more at home with diversity and creative exploration of truth. Of course we need both. It is not that we must abandon reason, and R. S. Thomas constantly struggled with the tension between mind and heart, but that we have to adjust to a world where reason is not regarded as the preeminent path to apprehending the truth about God and the world. We are the inheritors of the recent Christian past, which sought to communicate the gospel in a world at home with the dominance of reason. We are in transition from that position and need to find, or rediscover, other ways of knowing and communicating.

In *The Prodigal Project: Journey into the Emerging Church*, Mike Riddell, Mark Pierson and Cathy Kirkpatrick speak of their dislocation from the church in which they had been nurtured and their search for another way of being church. Along with many in the movements who are seeking to find an alternative way to engage with Christianity and express their faith in a way appropriate to our times, they identify the different cultural climate in which we are now living as being an important issue. They speak of that tension between heart and head. 'It's not that rationality is wrong or unnecessary. However there has been a growing understanding that it represents one approach to relating to the world, which on its own is insufficient to make sense of life. In particular, resistance has grown against *rationalism*, the elevation of reason to a position of authority which it has no right to occupy... There are important aspects of reality which the mind struggles to process, and at such points we may gladly confess its inadequacy, while not dispensing with its service entirely' (2000: 22).

But it is not only recently that the difficulties of a theoretical approach have been felt. In 1955 *The Cross in the Old Testament* by Wheeler Robinson was reprinted from material originally published early in the twentieth century. In this, he said, 'One great difficulty many have felt in regard to the Atonement is its apparent artificiality. God is conceived as allotting so much suffering for so much sin by a more or less arbitrary act. ... If we want reality, we must pay its price in facing complexity and difficulty and, it may be, unanswered questions' (1955: 109,110).

The theoretical approach seeks to eliminate the complexity, the mystery. It seeks to formulate how we can enter into a life free from oppressive powers or guilt and how this works. It correctly identifies that things are not right in this world but seeks to nail down precisely the remedy. We appreciate that sometimes there is a need to atone. We understand how it is for Amir in *The Kite Runner* who needs to find a way to work through his sins, to demonstrate his deep regret for what he did, and find a way to live a good life in the future. But what if the offence is so great that no action by the guilty one can make up for the crime? The Christian instinct is somehow that the death and resurrection of Christ is at the heart of unlocking that mystery, providing release and absolving the guilty one. But how to explain this? A theory may not be the best way.

Christabel Bielenberg, of Anglo/Irish descent, married a German lawyer Peter in 1934 and became a German national. They lived in Germany and when the darkness of the Second World War descended on them, they, along with many of their friends, resisted the Nazi propaganda and were opposed to what was being done in their name. After the failed plot against Hitler on 20th July 1944, Peter was arrested due to his association with those implicated in the plot, and was sent to Ravensbrück. Christabel told her story in *The Past is Myself* (1984). With great courage, she asked to be interviewed by the SS, believing that it might help to gain Peter's release. Remarkably, it did succeed. On her way home from her mission, not at that stage knowing the outcome, she had a long train journey ahead of her. She found herself sharing the same compartment as an SS officer.

Christabel was obviously a remarkable woman, and some quality in her must have communicated itself to that officer. The two of them were alone in the carriage and Christabel was at the point of exhaustion and collapse through strain and lack of food. The carriage was dark; she had only seen him once in a sudden shaft of light and observed the twitch distorting his face. As the night wore on he told her, as a voice coming out of the darkness, of the atrocities he had committed and how he was haunted by some of the events, of the little Jewish boy who asked if he was standing up straight enough – as he was about to shoot him. He had tried to get killed, the SS officer said, but each time his comrades had fallen but he was left standing:

'You are silent, *Gnädige Frau*? You are horrified at my story?' He seemed very near. 'No – no,' my own voice from somewhere far away; it seemed no longer my own. 'I am not horrified, I think I pity you, for you have more on your conscience than can be absolved by your death.'

And suddenly, for a second time, the fogs cleared and it was as if Adam's and Carl's dying and Peter's imprisonment seemed a splendid, glowing, real thing, absolutely necessary and right. 'But others have died and may have to die for you,' I heard myself murmuring. I do not know if he heard, as I was already nearly asleep. The train rumbled rhythmically onwards into the night. Totteridge, where I was born – a village church – a small Chris collecting her weekly text at children's service. Miss Osborne at the organ. 'He died that we might be forgiven. He died to make us good. He died – He died – '

I awoke twice before reaching Tuttlingen. Once, when the train jerked to a stop at a half-lit station, I realized that I was warmer and that my head was resting on something hard and uncomfortable. The man had moved and was sitting beside me, his greatcoat was over my knees and my head had fallen on to his shoulder. His SS shoulder tabs had been pressing into my cheek. In the half-light I saw his face for the second time: perhaps I had been mistaken about the twitching nerve; it looked peaceful enough now anyway, almost childlike. His hand, with the signet ring of the SS, was resting on mine, and as I moved it closed with an almost desperate grip and then relaxed (1984: 251-253).

In some way, the death of those who had resisted Hitler, the death of Christ, had absolved that German SS officer. The tale is told in a dreamlike way, between waking and sleeping, and has intuitive understanding but not theoretical explanation. We step on the edge of a great mystery and a great horror, and imaginative language is needed so that we can just feel the wind of something beyond our understanding as it passes by.

Perhaps there have always been those who knew that these deep truths cannot find complete and final expression in theory and it is that we are only now beginning to listen to them, hear and see how they apprehend reality. The artists, the story tellers and the poets have known how it is all along. But our society is only just catching up with these alternative ways of exploring truth. As always happens, we read the biblical texts through our own cultural lenses, and as we begin to see our 'modernist' lenses for what they are, we also see that what we thought were propositional statements in the biblical text were in fact speaking in the language of story and poetry.

The True Wilderness by Harry Williams (1965) is a collection of sermons majoring on the theme of crucifixion and resurrection, most of which were delivered in the academic environment of the Chapel of Trinity College, Cambridge. Williams was not setting out to devalue the contribution that academic theology brings. But understanding things at an intellectual level is not enough. He, too, was exploring that interface between mind and heart, particularly in relation to the Easter events. He found that he had been through some sort of conversion experience in which he could no longer speak of things which he did not know from personal experience. 'What was withheld from me was the ability to transmit second-hand convictions whatever their source, orthodox, modernist, or non-Christian. All I could speak of were those things which I had proved true in my own experience by living them and knowing them at first hand... There is nothing unusual about it. The same thing is done by every genuine artist in any medium. And had it not been done by St Paul and St John, not to mention Christ Himself, there would be no Christianity at all' (1965: 9).

Williams also recognizes that we do need theories, but they are not appropriate to all aspects of life. 'Civilization itself depends upon the capacity of the intellect to systematize its experience. But there are areas of human life where explanatory systems can falsify as well as illuminate' (1965: 10). Take relationships, for example, he suggests. Psychological theory can help up to a point but the complexity of human life cannot be reduced to a theory, without remainder. When we want to understand more, we do not turn to the textbook, but to the novelist and the poet. 'Here we find a point of view certainly. A general outlook on life. But it lacks the mathematical completeness and the neat coherence of an abstract theory and leaves us with all sorts of loose ends. For the novelist and the poet, if they know their job, are not constructing theorems. They are trying to give expression to life as they have known it in their own experience, mysterious, many-coloured and often inconsistent' (1965: 10).

It is the raggedness of life that the poet sees, the lived reality that tears apart the neat explanations. The atonement theories we have examined all have elements which show that reason and explanation alone are not sufficient when confronted with the crucifixion and resurrection of Christ. We have seen that the spirit of our times is moving away from the dominance of reason, a factor anticipated by those in previous generations with the appropriate sensitivity. Our ability to communicate and appropriate the Christian faith is compromised if we hang on tenaciously to the old ways of knowing. We need to open ourselves up to the creative voices that have been wrestling with the dilemmas and experiences and provide an imaginative language with which to see the world and God afresh. Poetry is one of those voices. In the next chapter we will explore how and why poetry might be able to help us.

Chapter Two
Poetry and the exploration of religious truth

What is poetry? We may feel that we instinctively know when we are faced with poetry rather than prose, but defining poetry is far more problematic. The book *Studying Poetry* commences with the poem 'Mona Lisa', with which W. B. Yeats had opened his anthology of poetry (Matterson and Jones, 2000: 2). Nothing too remarkable about that, one would think, *except* that this 'poem' started life as a piece of prose by Walter Pater and it was Yeats who converted it into poetry. How would the reader have known it was now poetry? There are clues, say Matterson and Jones, which include placing it in a book of poetry; presenting it as a self-contained unit with a title; there is a parallelism of form and structure; the lines are shorter and capitalized and have an internal rhythm (2000: 2). (These features are not a definitive summation of poetry and features can be abandoned and it does not therefore automatically cease to be poetry.) Matterson and Jones then go on to say that when the reader picks up these clues, realizes they have poetry and not prose before them, something happens to the reader, who then brings a different kind of attention to the text (2000: 3). Poetry requires and expects a response, a particular type of involvement, from the reader.

It is the heightened sense of reader response that makes poetry so suitable for the exploration of religious truth. We have already seen that intellectual understanding is insufficient on its own to appropriate religious truth, to make it your own. 'Christian truth .... must be in the blood as well as in the brain' as H. A. Williams says (1965: 8). Poetry calls forth from the reader something more, which has its springs in the imagination. R. S. Thomas says, 'My work as a poet has to deal with the presentation of imaginative truth. Christianity also seems to me to be a presentation of imaginative truth ... People no doubt are worried by the use of the word imagination, because imagination to many people has a fictional connotation, fictional overtones. Of course, I'm using the word imagination in its Coleridgean sense, which is the highest means known to the human psyche of getting into contact with the ultimate reality; imaginative truth is the most immediate way of presenting ultimate reality to a human being' (1972b: 53,54).

In his Introduction to the *Penguin Book of Religious Verse* (1963b), R. S. Thomas explores further the common ground between religion and poetry. Drawing again on Coleridge, Thomas says: 'The nearest we approach to God, he [Coleridge] appears to say, is as creative beings. The poet, by echoing the primary imagination, recreates. Through his work he forces those who read him to do the same, thus bringing them nearer the primary imagination themselves, and so, in a way, nearer to the actual being of God as displayed in action' (1963b: 8). So the reader is required to become a participant in the creative act of the poet, and thus grow nearer to the Creator, and this action has drawn on the wells of imagination and touches a deeper way of understanding than reason alone can provide.

William V. Davis supports this perception that poetry takes us to further reaches of our ability to appropriate that which is beyond, to ultimate reality, to God. It becomes part of our being, not something, or someone, we can hold at an intellectual distance. Poetry is a way in which that which is beyond becomes present to us but also allows that which is beyond to be presented, told about, communicated, to others. Davis says, 'through poetry (and only through poetry?) we are able to *present* (i.e., to make present or to represent) that experience [of ultimate reality]' (2007: 44).

Paul Avis speaks similarly of the avenue that the creative imagination gives to accessing God. He speaks of his 'conviction that the creative human imagination is one of the closest analogies to the being of God. The mystery of imagination points to and reflects the mystery of God. As Coleridge (among others) suggested, human imaginative creativity is an echo, a spark, of the divine creativity that is poured out in the plenitude of creation. Religious thinkers as different as St Augustine and William Blake have ... pictured God as a poet or artist who delights to reveal himself through the forms of the imagination: in the poetic and the symbolic' (Avis, 1999, ix).

Both R. S. Thomas and Paul Avis refer to Coleridge's explanation of imagination. Coleridge gives his definition of imagination in his *Biographia Literaria*. 'The primary IMAGINATION I hold to be the living Power and prime Agent of all human Perception, and as a repetition in the finite mind of the eternal act of creation in the infinite I AM. The secondary I consider as an echo of the former, co-existing with the conscious will, yet still as identical with the primary in the *kind* of its agency and differing only in *degree*, and in the *mode* of its operation' (quoted in Barth, 2001: 18).

It is clear from this that the imagination is not some form of escapism that has no relationship to reality. It is the ability, found in all to some extent but shaped and offered to us by the creative artist, to touch and feel

11

and understand that which is beyond words, but is the prime mover in our world. It is evident therefore the imagination that comes to expression in poetry is well suited, even essential, to the conveyance of religious truth.

As Barth says: 'In short, one can claim, in Coleridgean terms, that it is only imagination that can bring us to the full encounter with religious reality, because it is only symbolic language that resists the human drive for clarity and determinateness. The divine, the numinous, the transcendent, can never be encompassed by the clarity of "consequent Reasoning." It can only be intimated, guessed at, caught out of the corner of the eye; and for this, only the ambiguity of symbolic utterance will serve' (2001: 28).

The religious truth we are particularly wrestling with in this book is that which lies in and through the crucifixion and resurrection. The suggestion is that poetry is well suited to the exploration of the Easter events because it does not deal with systematic explanation, unlike atonement theory. But it hints at things, gives allusive reference and this stimulates and appeals to the imagination. Coleridge shows us that imagination is not some peripheral ability that we can easily dispense with in the pursuit of the understanding of the divine, but is in fact completely central to that pursuit. As R. S. Thomas has said, the work of the poet is the presentation of imaginative truth. And as poetry expects and demands a response, the imaginative truth can be appropriated by the reader.

So if the reader response is so significant in poetry, what features are there in poetry that call this forth? One outstanding feature is that it is memorable. R. S. Thomas says 'I am deploying language at a higher tension, in a more concise and memorable way than when writing prose... I am drawing on resources of resonance and memorability which are of the fibre of the language as it has been formed over the centuries' (1990b: 48). The point that poetry is something that the mind seems to hold onto is an important one because it allows echoes to reverberate in the mind and the imagination is exercised, after the reading has been completed. The words stay with the reader, perhaps buried for a while but ready to be called to mind again at an appropriate trigger.

The memorability lies not just in the particular words used but in the sound patterns they evoke. R. S. Thomas, in his lecture 'The Making of a Poem' (in *Selected Prose*, 1995b: 86) says 'there must be some kind of music which one is after, and indeed isn't this what makes poetry memorable?' For R. S. Thomas the process of making a poem found its origin in the first line that would come into his head, 'a line with its particular stresses and its particular scansion, sets the rhythm and pattern for the whole poem.

This links it up for me with all that has been written about the dance of life, the rhythm of life, the music of the spheres, the eternity of art, and all that sort of thing' (1995b: 87). This seems to be something within people that responds to the rhythm and cadence of poetry, whether at a conscious or subconscious level, so that sound and content become fused and the words live on, vibrating in the mind and body.

Another feature that requires the reader to take an active part is ambiguity. Ambiguity is of the essence of poetry, allowing multiple meanings to be held together at the one time. A theory requires an explanation that is understood in one particular way, but poetry delights in multiple meanings. R. S. Thomas says 'What I've tried to do, in my own sort of simple way as I've got older, is to try to operate on more than one level, to try to bring ambivalence and so on into the phrases' (1983b: 46). One of the ways he does this is in his masterful use of punning, so that you get, for each word or phrase, more than one meaning or line of thought.

The ability to retain multiple meanings is also enhanced by enjambment, a device that R. S. Thomas typically employs. This is where the meaning continues from one line of poetry to the next line or stanza and the unusual line breaks can have the effect of putting an emphasis on a word or phrase that would otherwise have passed unnoticed. A different understanding of what is being said is fleetingly experienced, before the succeeding line resolves it. But this undercurrent remains in the memory, pulling in a different direction from the whole, keeping alive a sense of ambiguity.

Irony requires the alert attention of the reader. What the words appear to say is in fact undercut by the intention of the writer, and this device brings a spotlight onto the surface proposal. The truth as it emerges becomes a wry truth. But of course it is possible to miss the irony and to take the text as it is read. Thomas comments 'I think there's a certain amount of misunderstanding of my work, a lot of my work is ironic' (1983b: 40). He uses irony in particular to challenge our preconceptions about God. If, however, this poetry is not understood as ironic, then the views represented can be thought to be Thomas's own, rather than those he wishes to challenge. Thomas asserts: 'I'm really being derisive about men's ideas of God... I believe in God, I'm trying to show how people sometimes attempt to pin down this, this Being Who's not a Being' (1983b: 40). The poet does however reserve the right to be inconsistent, to try out different positions, so it has to be said that it is not always easy to discern the presence of irony as opposed to contrasting views held in sincerity at the time (1997a: 79).

But it is metaphor that is perhaps the single most significant feature of poetry that allows religious truth to be appropriated. However if Thomas's readership had misunderstood his deployment of irony, Thomas believed that there had been an even more fundamental misunderstanding with regard to his references to metaphor in connection with the resurrection of Christ. In the John Ormond television documentary about the poet, R. S. Thomas said that '[t]he message of the New Testament is poetry. Christ was a poet, the New Testament is a metaphor, the Resurrection is a metaphor' (1972b: 53). In the Introduction to *Autobiographies*, Jason Walford Davies remarks that 'R. S. has often been attacked for his New Theology view that Christ's resurrection is essentially a 'metaphor'... Does he therefore not believe it happened literally?' (1997a: xvi). Barry Morgan mentions that R. S. Thomas described the Resurrection and Incarnation as 'only metaphors' (2006: 49).

On a number of occasions R. S. Thomas referred to that Ormond documentary and attempted to clarify what he meant. In answer to the question Lethbridge put to him, namely, 'You said you consider the Christian message a metaphor, but is it only a metaphor?', R. S. Thomas replies 'No. Well, I used the word metaphor in that context because of language. Language is symbolic. That is, our only medium of contact with Christianity is through the Gospels, which are language. The disciples, the evangelists, are trying to tell us about their experience' (1983b: 55). R. S. Thomas further elaborates on this in his interview with Molly Price-Owen and says :'[W]e have to take their account in language but there are aspects of language which are most successfully conveyed by metaphor and the risen Christ, the resurrection to me, as I said, is metaphor, it's an attempt to convey an experience of a kind of new life, an eruption of the deity into ordinary life, a lifting up of ordinary life into a higher level and this sort of thing' (2001: 98).

R. S. Thomas repeatedly stresses that the resurrection experience of the disciples comes to us through language and that his discussion is in that context. He certainly understood that the first Christians experienced something, but when that 'something' is beyond normal experience, language is strained in the telling. Resurrection terminology was available to the first disciples to convey that the person who was dead was now 'alive'. But the word 'resurrection' was formulated prior to the actual experience of seeing the 'risen' Christ. And what does 'alive' mean, when we are not simply stating that all the features of the previous existence continue in exactly the same way?

The Old Testament gives only hints at a belief in a full and undiminished life beyond the grave. There is, it is true, the undesirable and mysterious place of Sheol, which is neither heaven or hell as later understood, but is a place to which the dead go to live, if such a term can be used, a shady insubstantial life; it is a place from which to be delivered (Ps 30: 3). There is also the narrowly missed opportunity to eat from the tree of life, which was debarred to the first humans after they had eaten the forbidden fruit from the tree of knowledge. The offer here was of immortality rather than resurrection from the dead (Gen 2:4-3:24, cf. James Barr, *The Garden of Eden and the Hope of Immortality*, 1992).

It is Ezekiel who talks of resurrection. However this is referring to the nation rising again from the valley of dry bones to become a vibrant nation again, rather than an individual resurrection (Ezekiel 37: 1-14). Later, under persecution, the concept developed that the individual dead might indeed rise to new life – or to a less desirable prospect, depending on the life they had lived here (Daniel 12: 2). The apocalyptic work of Daniel is concerned with issues of justice. If this life is all there is, what of those who have been faithful to God but are martyred for their pains? The mention of resurrection belongs in the context of deliverance where God's people have been oppressed. The Old Testament resurrection language was born in the crucible of faith, founded on the character of the God in whom they believed.

When Jesus speaks to the Sadducees, who were conservative traditionalists who did not believe in resurrection and thus baited him with a trick question, he makes it clear that the risen bodies are not the same as those experienced in this life (Mark 12: 18-25). Caird says that: 'When Paul preached at Corinth the gospel of resurrection, he was apparently quite unprepared for the literalism with which his words were received, and he had to be at great pains to reassure them that the resurrection body would not be a body of flesh and blood (1 Cor. 15: 35-50)' (1980: 247). So although the language of 'bodies' may be used it is far from clear exactly what is envisaged. And when the disciples met Jesus after Easter Sunday, resurrection language was available to them to give expression to the experience, but that language had been developed in the context of trust in God's faithfulness, rather than in a context of literal description of a previous occurrence. Nobody had previously seen a 'resurrection body' of the kind that the disciples believed they had seen in the risen Christ.

So for R. S. Thomas to say that the disciples experienced something and the language they used was metaphorical, is not to make a statement about the truthfulness or otherwise of their claims, but to alert us to the difficulties of describing something never previously experienced precisely in this way, although hoped for in the providence of God. As Caird says, 'literal and metaphorical are terms which describe types of language, and the type of language we use has very little to do with the truth or falsity of what we say and with the existence or non-existence of the things we refer to' (1980: 131).

Janet Martin Soskice, in her definitive book *Metaphor and Religious Language* (1985), helpfully clarifies the position of metaphor and its relation to truth. She gives as a working definition of metaphor that it is a '*figure of speech* whereby we speak about one thing in terms which are seen to be suggestive of another' (my emphasis) (1985: 15).

Metaphor is sometimes regarded, she says, as a 'decorative way of saying what could be said literally' or for 'the affective impact it has' but the most productive theory is that which sees 'metaphor as a unique cognitive vehicle enabling one to say things that can be said in no other way' (1985: 24). It is this last definition that R. S. Thomas is using.

Soskice then says that '[o]ne often hears ... talk of 'mere metaphor' or of something being 'only metaphorical' or 'only metaphorically true', or in contradistinction, 'literally true''(1985:67). This betrays a false understanding of metaphor. She explains why: 'A given truth may be expressed by a metaphor, may perhaps only be expressed by using the metaphor, but this is not to say that it exemplifies a sort of 'metaphorical truth' distinguishable from and inferior to 'literal truth'. We may warn someone, 'Watch out! That's a live wire', but even if we think that wires are not literally 'live' we do not add 'but of course that is only metaphorically true.' It is true and it is expressed with the use of a metaphor' (1985: 70). Metaphor is the meat and drink of the poet and metaphor opens up for the reader possibilities for exploration and new understandings. It is a work which is not finished. For unlike a literal description there are always further insights to be gleaned as the metaphor is explored in different ways. It is living and dynamic language.

'Poets' says Sally McFague, 'use metaphor all the time because they are constantly speaking about the great unknowns – mortality, love, fear, joy, guilt, hope, and so on. Religious language is deeply metaphorical for the same reason and it is therefore no surprise that Jesus' most characteristic form of teaching, the parables, should be extended metaphors' (1982: 15). To talk of that which we do not know or something completely new we need a language bridge to stretch from the familiar to the unfamiliar: 'Thinking metaphorically means spotting a thread of similarity between two dissimilar objects, events, or whatever, one of which is better known than the other, and using the better known one as a way of speaking about the lesser known' (1982: 15).

This helps to explain why R. S. Thomas said that Christ was a poet and the New Testament is a metaphor. In talking of things that are straining our understanding, beyond literal description, metaphor is not only the best language, but the only language that we can use. It is not some inferior form of truth, but the avenue to a greater truth than our finite minds can comprehend. But it requires the work and involvement of the reader and hearer for it to be appropriated. It requires the exercise of the imagination.

There is a fluidity in the exercise of the poetic imagination that does not require things to be firmly nailed down, other interpretations eliminated. So it seems possible that people who have different perspectives on the cross can still find within the same poetry some resonance of their own. The poem, like metaphor, does not mean one thing and one thing only. In a similar vein, R. S. Thomas suggests this is the strength of Christianity, that it 'maintains a reciprocal relationship with the culture of its converts. The main reason for this surely is the poetic nature of its original message, which allows itself to be interpreted and expressed in an infinite number of ways' (*Selected Prose*, 1995b: 69).

From all this we can see that poetry has possibilities for exploring crucifixion and resurrection which an explanation, a theory, does not possess. With its involvement of the reader, its encouragement of the imagination, its highly condensed language carrying an excess of meaning, its memorability, ambiguity, irony and metaphor, what could be a better vehicle for enriching our appropriation of the mystery of life and the Christian faith than poetry?

And perhaps there is a further way poetry can be of use in relation to appropriating ideas centring round the cross. James Hopewell (1987: 58) utilizes the literary narrative theory of Northrop Frye to gain insights into the different worldviews that characterize separate congregations. Frye suggests that Western literature is always oriented to one of four compass points of comedy, romance, tragedy and irony, or a position between these points.

Hopewell uses this theory in relation to congregations, stressing that they will have a particular orientation. He uses the picture of a church he was involved with which had its building on a hill, with windows on all four walls, so the congregation could arrange themselves to look out in any direction. He speculates on what the choice of direction would signify. 'To the east, with its promise of dawn after a dark night, envision works of comedy ... Move around the circle ... until reaching the south and its pure romantic interpretations ...The pure tragedies meet the setting western sun ... Put the ironies in the northern night and cold' (1987: 67). Although you can have combinations of near points of the compass, you do not have opposites together in the one narrative.

Can poetry however hold together opposites? In a narrative, comedy may, indeed probably will, have elements of tragedy but the final resolution is determined as an upbeat outcome. Conversely tragedy may have elements of comedy, but the comedy will be subservient to the eventual tragic outcome. The narrative of the crucifixion and resurrection is that the outcome is not tragic, however it might have seemed on the journey. But can poetry hold together in the imagination both comedy and tragedy so that one is not subservient to the other? When we come to examine R. S. Thomas's poetry there are certain poems that seem to open up this possibility. The suggestion that the poet might hold together two opposing points of the compass is indicated by Rowan Williams' poem, 'Deathship', written in memory of R. S. Thomas. The last two lines read: 'At dawn, somewhere westward, / the boat flares in a blaze of crying birds' (2002: 89).

William Blake was fascinated by opposites or 'contraries' and believed that they needed to be held in tension; that the one should not dissolve into the other, or that the the other should not negate the one. Jonathan Roberts explains:

Most readers first encounter Blake's poetry through the *Songs of Innocence and of Experience*. The two sets of poems are based on culturally familiar categories whereby 'innocence' and 'experience' stand in a linear relationship to each other. Traditionally, individuals are thought to move, chronologically, from the state of innocence to the state of experience, as in the change from childhood to adulthood. Conventionally, one state replaces the other, and the two cannot be concurrent. Blake's challenge to this paradigm is evident in the subtitle of the combined edition of the *Songs* which reads, 'Shewing the Two Contrary States of the Human Soul'. In different editions of the *Songs* he shifts poems between categories because, in Blake's view, contrary states exist not in linear sequence, but in parallel: they are simultaneous (2007: 39).

The world contains what seem to be opposites but the presence of both is required, even though this feels to be counterintuitive at times. One aspect seems 'better' than the other so we would like to eliminate the opposing state. So, for example, reason, which had become pre-eminent in Blake's time, was at fault not intrinsically, but because it had assumed a tyrannical position. When brought back into a proper tension, heart and mind are positive, dialectical positions.

The world as we know it has both light and dark, literally and metaphorically, and there are times when we would like to obliterate the dark. But the darkness is part of the created world and is something with which the poet has to wrestle. Much of R. S. Thomas's poetry is concerned with this theme. Blake's 'The Tyger', part of the *Songs of Experience*, poses the question 'Did he who made the Lamb make thee?' Can the 'Tyger' radiating a burning intensity in the 'forests of the night' create the same sense of delight in the creator as the Lamb? The tiger and the lamb seem to be opposites, but do we need these opposites?

Tracy Chevalier's novel '*Burning Bright*' (2007) seems at first to be only peripherally concerned with William Blake, who is the neighbour of the family who moved to Lambeth following a tragedy in their rural Dorset. But the story is an enactment of Blake's 'contraries', as the children Maisie (Margaret) and Jem get to know their new neighbour and form a friendship with the 'experienced' local girl Maggie (Margaret). Town and countryside are opposites but each have qualities the other lacks, the innocent Maisie turns out not to be so innocent, and the experienced Maggie is touchingly innocent at times. All the children grow to love and respect, with a certain awe and wonder, Mr Blake. When the country family eventually leave London to return home, the Blakes shelter the pregnant Maisie until just shortly before her delivery when Maggie takes her home to her family. William Blake gives Maggie two books, one for her and one for Jem.

But Maggie gets the books, *Songs of Innocence* and *Songs of Experience*, muddled up and cannot remember which is for Jem – and they are unable to decide by then which one is most appropriate for whom:

They looked down at their books in the coming dark. Then Maggie leaned over the page of Jem's book. 'Is that a tiger?'

Jem nodded, and peered at the words. ' "Tyger tyger –" '

' "Burning bright," ' Maggie joined in, to his surprise.

> In the forests of the night
> What immortal hand or eye
> Could frame thy fearful symmetry?

'Maisie taught me that,' she added. 'I can't read – yet.'

'Maisie taught you?' Jem pondered this, wondering how much his sister had changed from her stay in London, 'What's "symmetry"?'

'Dunno – you'll have to ask her.' (2007: 384)

But Maggie is a city girl so has to return to London, whereas Jem is a country boy. But they feel the books belong together so they each offer to let the other have their volume, and come and visit so that they can see the two together. Maggie insists that Jem should keep both and she will come and visit, no small gesture as she had found the countryside a terrifying place, much more unnerving to her than the city.

Jem laughed and took her hand. 'Then you would have to learn to cross this field alone.'

'Not if you came to meet the coach.' (2007: 386)

Perhaps there is a deep truth here, which the analytical mind resists but the creative mind can encompass, that the 'contraries' of crucifixion and resurrection are eternally simultaneously present and that this runs through the world like the writing in a stick of rock. 'Contraries' form part of our world and we need to learn how to hold these together: to realize that songs of innocence and songs of experience are two volumes of the same book, as indeed they became; to learn how to take the hand of the other and meet the other so that the one is not left to 'cross this field alone'.

There are voices in the Old Testament giving expression to the tension of opposites, 'contraries', which agonize over, wrestle with, the dilemmas raised by a world believed to have been created 'good' but demonstrating evidence to the contrary. In the next chapter we will explore these voices.

Chapter Three
The counter-testimony of the Psalmist and Job

Molly Price-Owen asked R. S. Thomas, in an interview conducted in his old age, whether he had a favourite book of the Bible. Thomas replied 'It's a difficult question. I certainly like *Job* – *Job* is a very grand conception. I am in a way a Biblical Christian, I suppose. Leaving out all that tedious sort of rubbish you know, about *Leviticus* and all this sort of thing, I would go along with being described as a kind of Bible Christian. I think some of the things in the *Old Testament* are really sublime, some of the conceptions there and *Job* is certainly one of the books' (2001: 99).

Earlier in R. S. Thomas's life, in the 1970s, John Ormond made a television documentary about the poet. During the film 'R. S. Thomas is seen entering the church. The strains of a hymn are heard from outside. Then we hear the poet reading Psalm 90' (1972b: 55). R. S. Thomas then continues his conversation with his interviewer John Ormond and says 'Well, of course, the great thing about the liturgy of the Christian church and the Bible and the New Testament is that the language is a product of a high stage of literary culture; and language when it is being employed at this level has a wonderfully reverberative power and it doesn't matter how often one repeats or listens to language at this level, its reverberative power is more or less inexhaustible. And, therefore repeating – every day if you like – such psalms as the 23rd or the 90th Psalm, one is allowing oneself to be stimulated or to be reached by these overtones implicit in this liturgical language' (1972b: 55).

So we see that the Bible, or at least certain parts, had a deep significance for R. S. Thomas. It was a living text and shaped him. As we noted earlier, poetry has the quality of memorability so that the vibrations resound in the mind and heart after the reading is finished. It is interesting that the two books, Job and Psalms, are both poetry. The language stimulates the imagination and there are endless possibilities residing in the text, so that even if you return to them on a daily basis, Thomas suggests, you will not have exhausted their riches.

Ancient Poetry of the Spirit (1997b) is a selection of psalms taken from the Authorized Version and published by Lion. R. S. Thomas wrote the Foreword to this volume and comments how the words from the AV translation 'so long have reverberated in the English psyche'. They are somewhere we can 'turn to have our feelings eloquently expressed for us in our own attempts to find God and glorify him'. And 'The Psalms were Hebrew poetry, the expression of a nation's sorrow and exultation in its search for God' (1997b: 7).

The Psalms were meaningful writings for R. S. Thomas, as was the book of Job, so we will look further at these two biblical texts. In particular we will focus on the insights of the Old Testament scholar Walter Brueggemann as there seems to be a great affinity between Brueggemann's understanding of these texts and the edgy, questioning, subversive – but also affirmative – approach of R. S. Thomas. It was sorrow and exultation that Thomas particularly identified as being characteristic of the search for God in the psalms. It is sorrow and exultation that we find in R. S. Thomas's own poetry as he too searches for God. We begin to see that there is a dynamic present in this search, and that crucifixion and resurrection is not, so to speak, a one off event, but rather has a continuity that stretches back into elements of the Old Testament record.

However, not everybody sees the world in the same way, and this is also true of the voices we hear in the Old Testament. We have perhaps fallen prey in the Western modern Christian world to the need to systematize our faith and eliminate those discordant voices that speak against a dominant understanding. But the Old Testament (which in a different register is the Hebrew Scriptures) allows the different voices to co-exist and for the ambiguous text to remain. Truth claims need to be explored from more than one angle and Walter Brueggemann uses law court imagery to suggest that, as in the pursuit of truth in a law court you hear the story from more than one witness, so also the Hebrew way is to allow those different testimonies to be heard and to hold them together. There may be a dominant story or testimony, but the voices challenging that way of understanding will not be silenced or thrown out of court. So Brueggemann says:

> The cross-examination is not intended by Israel to obliterate the core testimony. In the disputatious propensity of Israel, rather, core testimony and cross-examination belong to each other and for each other in an ongoing exchange. Thus there will never be a "final" testimony in Israel that will not be subject to cross-examination. Nor will there ever be a cross-examination to which

the consensus testimony does not make a vigorous response ... As a result, it is evident that Israel's counter-testimony is not an act of unfaith. It is rather a characteristic way in which faith is practiced (1997: 317,318).

We need to hold in tension the core testimony, which speaks of God's sovereignty and faithfulness, and the counter-testimony, which tells of the hiddenness, ambiguity and negativity. It may be simpler for ecclesial authority to stick to the core testimony, to silence the problematic voices. However, as Brueggemann states, 'Such a process yields a coherent faith, but it requires mumbling through many aspects of lived experience that evoked the counter-testimony in the first place' (1997: 400). And it is precisely this challenge of lived experience that the poet R. S. Thomas brings to the debate: his is the Christian poetic voice of counter-testimony. As Brueggemann has argued, this is not an act of unfaith, but is the very nature of an authentic, living, truthful faith.

In *The Penguin Book of Religious Verse* edited by R. S. Thomas there is a section he designates as 'Nothing'. Thomas justifies the inclusion of these poems as follows: 'Poetry is born of the tensions set up by the poet's ability to be 'in uncertainties, mysteries, doubts, without any irritable reaching after fact and reason'. Without the section entitled 'Nothing' I feel that the contents of this anthology would have been incomplete and its poetry the poorer' (1963b: 11). Included in that section is William Blake's 'The Sick Rose', one of the poet's songs of experience. It is interesting that in the quotation to which Thomas refers, poetry is able to resist the need to find explanations which satisfy the reason, but is prepared to live with the 'uncertainties, mysteries, doubts'.

But it does not necessarily live quietly, or without protest. It is this ability to articulate and protest about the challenging issues of life in this world that we find in the poets/prophets of the Old Testament. To acquiesce in quiet conformity when a voice shouts within that things are not right, is surely not a healthy or truthful way of being. As Brueggemann says: 'Moreover, the loss of this standard practice of complaint and petition from theological perspective, which has entailed the loss of self-assertion over against Yahweh and the forfeiture of counter-testimony about Yahweh, is precisely what has produced "false selves," both in an excessively pietistic church that champions deference and in an excessively moralistic, brutalizing society that prizes conformity and the stifling of rage' (1997: 475,476). The poetry of R. S. Thomas does give expression to the mental agony produced in the sensitive person when involved in or witness to a suffering that seems intrinsic to the world and therefore to be, in some measure, God's fault. But the language he often uses to explore these difficult issues is the language of the cross, thus taking it back into the heart of God. It is this ability to talk of the absence of God, the culpability of God, the perplexities of a world where the good suffer and the wicked prosper, yet hold this in a faith context, that we find in the Old Testament psalmist. We therefore turn now to examine in more detail Brueggemann's analysis of the message we find in the Psalms.

In *The Message of the Psalms* (1984) Brueggemann suggests that we can loosely categorize the psalms into three broad groups. First we find the psalms of orientation, which speak of a world that is ordered, coherent, reliable and joyful. The people who can speak such psalms without a qualm are drawn from the stratum of society where law works for them rather than against them, where prosperity marks their standing and favour in society, and where the people with power hear their voice. Or it is people in denial. Some people are socially and temperamentally comfortable with a God praised through psalms of orientation. Psalm 1, not surely placed accidentally as the opening psalm, is such a psalm of orientation. It asserts confidently that, 'The Lord watches over the way of the righteous / but the way of the wicked is doomed' (1: 6).

But into some lives and social groups comes a terrible disorientation. From these alienated, suffering, sorrowing and angry people, who yet believe this is a world where there is a God, come the psalms of disorientation. Life is not ordered, or if it is, it is not ordered aright, and out of lives torn apart with jagged edges, words of protest, confusion and petition come. (Psalms 89, 88, 22 and 90, which we will be considering shortly, come in this category.)

Lastly, however, there are the psalms of new orientation, such as Psalm 23. This is not a return to the old order of orientation, where there was no cloud on the horizon. These people have been through the storms, they know that life can be turned upside down and all that has been held dear, shredded. The new orientation is a gift of God. Out of the darkness, or even in the darkness, there is light. For 'the speaker and the community of faith are often surprised by grace, when there emerges in present life a new possibility that is inexplicable, neither derived nor extrapolated, but wrought by the inscrutable power and goodness of God. That newness cannot be explained, predicted, or programmed' (Brueggemann, 1984: 124).

Brueggemann suggests that this dynamic of orientation, disorientation and new orientation is one which the Christian will readily recognize. He writes: 'I have concluded at the end of the study (and not as a presupposition) that the shape and dynamic of the Psalms can most usefully be understood according to the theological framework of crucifixion and resurrection' (1984: 10). This is not thereby to turn the Psalms into a 'Christian' book, for it is Jewish through and through, but it identifies a walk with God that is profoundly disorienting at times but does have a resurrection hope shaped in the crucible of despair.

If we cast our minds back to the discussion of resurrection in chapter two, we noted there that resurrection language came painfully to birth in the Old Testament and inter-testamental period through the challenges of suffering. Surely a God who cared about his people could not allow them to be obliterated from this world, could not allow the covenant relationship of fidelity to be finally and irrevocably terminated by death? Resurrection faith is the outcome of a belief in, and an experience of, the God who can make all things new, even in this life.

When God can turn disorientation into a gratuitous and unexpected experience of life, can this not be projected into a new life beyond the grave? In this sense, resurrection belief is based on trust in the character of God. But the character of God is disputed in the Old Testament, and what causes the dispute are those occasions when observed reality confronts the inherited patterns of belief.

Psalm 89 starts confidently: 'I shall sing always of the loving deeds of the Lord; throughout every generation I shall proclaim your faithfulness' (v.1). The certainty of the Davidic covenant reassures the psalmist. Creation affirms the strength and faithfulness of God, and righteousness and faithfulness are foundational to his rule. The mood is joyful and secure, for God will keep the Davidic king safe. There is the recognition that if people are disobedient, punishment will follow, but this will not threaten the long-term security of the Davidic line.

Then, at verse 38, the mood changes – dramatically. In retrospect, all those earlier verses take on an ironic note. What has happened? Exile has happened. In no way is the suffering now endured commensurate with wrongs done. Where is the faithfulness of God now? 'Yet you have spurned your anointed one, you have rejected him and raged against him, you have renounced the covenant with your servant, defiled his crown and flung it to the ground' (vv 38,39).

Of this psalm, Brueggemann says in *Deep Memory Exuberant Hope*: 'Exile is Israel's large, defining act of suspicion. Israel will not lie about exile, will not lie to protect Yahweh, or to deceive itself. Israel will not lie about its circumstance, its loss, or its pain in order to protect large theological slogans. I stress this because my experience is that many Christians feel obligated somehow to protect God's honor at all costs, including the cost of denial' (1999: 53).

Sometimes the protest cannot be resolved and has to be left on the table. There are times when it seems that tragedy is an accurate description of life. The faith story may generally be one that speaks of a faithful God who brings new birth out of death but this cannot be assumed. Psalm 88 is such a psalm of despair. 'From childhood I have suffered and been near to death; I have borne your terrors, I am numb ... You have taken friend and neighbour far from me; darkness is now my only companion' (vv 15, 18). Not only is God no help, according to the psalmist, he is the cause of all the distress. The character of God cannot be assumed to right all wrongs and intervene to bring about a happy outcome. For some people, experience appears to show otherwise. The book of Psalms retains this counter-testimony of painful despair and does not try to explain, modify or expunge this record. It remains a stark challenge to any comfortable, comforting religion. Yet the psalm is still addressed to God, for this is part of the dialectic of faith.

But yet even in the darkest psalms, there can still be a movement towards a hope beyond hope. The evidence for delivery may not be apparent, but still there is some tenuous clinging to the God who can save. Psalm 22, the opening desperate words of which are found on the lips of the crucified Jesus (Mark 15: 34), speak of a profound abandonment. The psalmist tells of the mockery his faith receives in the light of his current plight. With deep irony, the passers by say 'He threw himself on the Lord for rescue; let the Lord deliver him, for he holds him dear!' (Ps 22: 8). Yet, despite his dire situation, the psalmist can say 'But I shall live for his sake' and succeeding generations will be able to say 'The Lord has acted' (22: 29,31).

Psalm 90, the psalm R. S. Thomas was reading in the John Ormond documentary, speaks of the transitory and ephemeral nature of human life compared with the enduring nature of God. Life, even the life not terminated prematurely, is short. 'Seventy years is the span of our life, eighty if our strength holds; at their best they are but toil and sorrow, for they pass quickly and we vanish' (v 10). Our destiny is 'dust' (v 3). But the dynamic comes into play that sorrow may be part of life, but so also is joy. 'Grant us days of gladness for the days you have humbled us, for the years when we have known misfortune' (v 15). Brueggemann comments of the psalm 'It could be that such a prayer in a time of disorientation is deception and denial. But I think not... The speaker has concluded that our situation is not finally defined by dust and grass' (1984: 115).

And then we come through to psalms of new orientation, which is not a tightly defined category, and it is debatable whether some psalms belong to the old orientation, before trouble arose, or to the new orientation when the faithfulness of God is celebrated but the sorrow at the heart of the world is recognized. It depends to a certain extent on whose are the lips speaking the words (Brueggemann 1984: 22,125).

But the new orientation comes as gift. These psalms are not about explanation; but grateful observation that such newness is experienced in a yet disordered world. It is not theory we are offered, but praise. 'The newness cannot be explained, predicted, or programmed. We do not know how such a newness happens any more than we know how a dead person is raised to new life, how a leper is cleansed, or how a blind person can see (cf. Luke 7: 22). We do not know; nor do the speakers of these psalms. Since Israel cannot explain and refuses to speculate, it can do what it does best. It can tell, narrate, recite, in amazement and gratitude, "lost in wonder, love, and praise"' (Brueggemann 1984: 124).

The second psalm that R. S. Thomas referred to in the Ormond documentary is Psalm 23. This is a psalm of confidence, but it is confidence in the face of real dangers and real difficulties. The speaker knows that there are valleys of deep darkness, that there are enemies around, that spirits can flag and require revival by refreshing pools and green grass. But in and through this, God gives blessing which is like an overflowing cup, imagery we will find R. S. Thomas picks up and develops in his poetry. There is a journey to be taken in God that goes by way of disorientation and comes through to a new orientation where God can still hold the person, despite the presence of enemies.

But the journey taken is not a linear one where the disorientation is left behind forever, never to be experienced again. The newness can also become stale and lacking in sustenance, if the experience becomes routine and institutionalized. Neither did Brueggemann wish to suggest that his framework was an explanatory theory which systemized all experience. He offered it instead 'simply as a way to suggest connections between life and speech' (1984: 22). The important thing here is that life is a constant check on the speech we make about God. The voices of counter-testimony will not let religious language become a closed system that cannot be overturned by life.

And it was the disorientation experienced in Job's life that led him to question, not the existence of God, but the character of God and the relationship with such a God. Brueggemann says that 'It is widely agreed that the Book of Job is Israel's most ambitious counter-testimony concerning the crisis of theodicy' (1997: 386). However Brueggemann then goes on to comment that for Israel, theodicy is not to 'justify the ways of God to man' as it is in the philosophical tradition, but in Israel, 'what is called theodicy is not explanation but protest' (1997: 739). R. S. Thomas in his poetry embodies the Christian response to the injustices and suffering that are experienced in the world. It is not difficult to see therefore why Thomas found Job to be such a profound work.

But it is also interesting that Brueggemann has identified the same dynamic of orientation, disorientation, new orientation that he found in the Psalms, to be present in the book of Job (1997: 489). The prologue and the epilogue to the book of Job are written in prose and may be based on a pre-existing story, but they now form an integral part of the book. In the prologue we are introduced to Job, an upright, prosperous, religiously observant man, well-respected and honoured on earth and in heaven. Except one day, as God sits in his heavenly council, the Adversary (or the Satan) suggests to God that it is not so surprising that Job is a God fearing man when life is so kind to him but, subject him to trials, and then it will really become apparent what is Job's motivation. God allows calamities to befall Job, but Job stands firm. Then, further incited by the Adversary, God allows Job himself, not just those around him and his property, to be smitten and we are then set up for the poetic dialogue that forms the majority of the book.

Job is visited by a band of 'comforters', or friends, who try to discern the purposes of God in Job's affliction. The difficulty is that they work from a theological presupposition that suffering and sin are so inextricably linked that if someone suffers they must have sinned: there is no place for innocent suffering in their scheme. Job must therefore be a sinner. Job disputes this vigorously and wishes to argue his case with God. He just wants his day in court, to be heard, and the implication is that if Job is found innocent then God must be guilty. Eventually God speaks, but the issues of Job's innocence are not addressed; he is simply confronted by the complexity of the creation. Neither is Job given information about the deliberations of the heavenly council that preceded his sufferings.

But perhaps Job had been pursuing the wrong tack, in that he intended a confrontation in which there were winners and losers? 'Would you dare deny that I am just, or put me in the wrong to prove yourself right? (40: 8) questions God. Indeed Job did intend to put God in the wrong to show that he himself was innocent, as he is working on the presupposition that God should crush all the wicked, and it seems that the theoretical construct although neat and comprehensive, having truth within it that sin and punishment are related, has become a totalizing explanation. Job, for all that he disputes with the 'comforters' the explanations they give of his suffering, is still working from the same supposition as them that sin and suffering are inseparably linked, but it is just that God has got it wrong in Job's case, because Job is innocent (Job Ch 31). If Job, says God ironically, was able to deal with all the wickedness in the world and obliterate it, then God would take his hat off to Job, metaphorically speaking (40: 9-14). The world turns out to be more complicated than Job had realized.

Then we come to the climax of the book, Job's final reply to God (42:1-6). Job had given an interim reply in 40:4,5 but there he confessed that he had nothing more to say. Such a resolution did not appear to be satisfactory, for God continued to speak. Job ultimately confesses that yes, he had spoken of things he did not understand, but having heard God he now sees. Then he adds, 'Wherefore I abhor myself, and repent in dust and ashes' 42:6, AV translation. What does that mean?

The fundamental premise of the book is that Job is innocent (1:8, 2:3). So why should he repent? Is it of arguing with God? But in the prose epilogue, God says to the friends that 'you have not spoken as you ought about me, as he has done' (42:8), so in fact Job is commended for his wrestling with God in speech. It appears that there is another way of translating and understanding verse 42:6. The two verbs, which the AV has translated as 'abhor' and 'repent', are to be understood as one action and therefore the object becomes 'dust and ashes' and the word 'myself' becomes superfluous. E. M. Good has translated the verse 'Therefore I despise and repent of dust and ashes' (1990: 171). It is no longer necessary to say I despise *myself* or I abhor *myself*. But we are still left with a puzzle. What does it mean to repent of dust and ashes?

The phrase 'dust and ashes' occurs in two other places in the Old Testament: Gen. 18: 27 and Job 30: 19. The Genesis reference is the story of Abraham confronting the Lord over issues of justice in relation to Sodom. Abraham challenges the Lord over the justice of wiping out a whole population when the innocent will suffer along with the guilty. Would God preserve Sodom if fifty innocent people could be found?

'Should not the judge of all the earth do what is just?' (v 25) challenges Abraham? Then when God agrees to pardon the city for the sake of fifty, Abraham asks the same question again and again, working his way down in stages from fifty to ten. Abraham is really pushing his luck, and he knows it. In the midst of this debate Abraham says 'May I make so bold as to speak to the Lord, I who am nothing but dust and ashes?'

How interesting that Abraham describes himself in terms of dust and ashes and yet he doesn't behave as though he is nothing – far from it! So although Abraham *says* he is but dust and ashes, is he not, through his encounter with God, in the experience of being heard by God, denying that designation?

Put this together with Job 30:19, prior to God's response, where Job says 'God himself has flung me down in the mud; I have become no better than dust and ashes'. Why did he at that stage see himself as dust and ashes? The answer is in the next verse where he says 'I call out to you, God, but you do not answer, I stand up to plead, but you keep aloof'. When God did not speak to him, Job felt like dust and ashes.

But the point is, Abraham had been answered by God: he was not dust and ashes. By the time we get to chapter 42, Job has been answered by God, he no longer needs to see himself as dust and ashes. So Job can 'repent' of dust and ashes, he can reject the assessment of himself as a bit of dirt.

In the prose epilogue, Job is restored to health and strength, and he is given double the fortune, beautiful daughters and a long life. But the story, which seemed to be about the problem of suffering, has not solved the theoretical problems. All we know now is that it is all more complicated than we thought, that the voice of counter-testimony is acknowledged and welcomed, and that in this complex world human beings, although limited in knowledge, are still valuable to God and recipients of his gratuitous bounty: they are not simply 'dust'. Which is the same conclusion we reached when thinking about Psalm 90.

The Book of Job turns out to be not so much a treatise on suffering but on the journey of a man who thought he understood the world and God, from a place of religious and material comfort, and was plunged into a disorientating world where all he thought he knew was challenged. He comes through to a place which does not deny his suffering, does not actually assure him of his innocence, but does assure him that God hears him. By the verbal link with Abraham, that great man of faith, we see Job too as a man of faith. In Jewish tradition the counter-testimony is part of faith.

William Blake, near the end of his life, completed a set of twenty-one Illustrations of the book of Job where he provides his interpretation of the story pictorially, but supplemented by verses from the Old and New Testament which provide an interpretive key to the pictures.

William Blake exercised a freedom in his interpretation of the biblical text and a freedom in his use of the wording of the text, amending it where he felt it was so required. He has, however, illustrated the story in such a way to show how Job moves, as a result of undergoing his trials, from a 'book religion' to one where there is an immediacy of encounter with God: a religion of the Spirit.

Plates 1 and 21 of Blake's Illustrations match the prologue and epilogue of the biblical book. In the first plate Job is sitting under a tree with his wife and family and open on his lap is the Bible. The family are at prayer and dutifully kneeling. In the foreground sheep are sleeping and on the sheltering tree hang unused musical instruments. He is a good, religiously observant man but there is something lacking as indicated by the text on the altar 'The Letter Killeth The Spirit giveth Life.'

When disasters afflict him, Job descends into a nightmare world. God is remote, Satan is all too present, and Job is tormented by evil dreams. What is noticeable about the figure of God is that it is the same figure as Job. This is a God created in Job's image, and it turns out to be a most frightening God. He has been worshipping an idol. The journey Blake's Job goes on is to bring him to the true God and to know this God in a new way. What this takes is for Job to move from his comfortable orientation into a hideously disorientating world.

The issue of Job turns out not to be the issue of suffering, which is never resolved, but the character of God and how we can know God in a world where suffering occurs. In the Vision of God, Plate 17, we have Blake's interpretation of Job 42: 1-6. God, still the same figure as Job, is no longer remote in heaven but stands before him in blessing. The verse above the clouds shows us how we are now to understand this likeness. 'We know that when he shall appear we shall be like him for we shall see him as He Is' (1 John 3:2). Job has been brought low but now is experiencing new orientation. At the top of the picture are the words 'He bringeth down to the Grave and bringeth up' (1 Sam. 2:6). He has experienced crucifixion and resurrection. And nowhere does Blake mention the verse 'Wherefore I abhor myself and repent in dust and ashes'! Job and his wife are composed and peaceful, kneeling respectfully but not cowering, unlike the friends who have their backs to God and fearfully hide their heads in their hands.

Blake imaginatively constructs a scene of Job with his new daughters in Plate 20. Job's arms are extended over them in blessing, echoing the gesture of God on the wall painting behind him. There are other scenes depicted in these wall paintings and it has been suggested that these show scenes from his trials (Wright, 1972: 49). Although Job has come through to a new place of blessedness, the paintings on the walls are an ever-present reminder that his new understanding came through a time of disorientation. He cannot return to the life he had before the trials came upon him.

The final plate, 21, the equivalent of the biblical epilogue, is a mirror image of the first plate, but with very significant differences. Job and his family are now standing up, the musical instruments have been taken down from the tree and are being played, the sheep are waking up, the church which obscured the sun in the first picture can no longer be seen and the dawn is breaking. 'Just and True are thy Ways' (Rev 15:3) are the words shown at the top right. The justice of God which had so much been in question in the book of Job, has been affirmed, despite all that has happened. But we have no explanation, only praise.

Suffering matters and it is right to wrestle with the problem intellectually. There are partial answers but there is no complete answer. As soon as we think we have a total solution, facts have to be manipulated to conform to our theory. The psalmist who endures disorientation protests against such theological conformity, as does the suffering Job. Questions of the competence, faithfulness, justice and compassion of God are raised. When the world seems unjust, God's character is on trial. The voices of counter-testimony will not be silenced by concerns about the audacity of speaking thus of God. The resolution however, where resolution comes (and this cannot be assumed) is not through an intellectual solution but through the assurance of presence and significance. God may have seemed absent, an abyss may have opened up, but the statement of faith is that the dynamic will lead through to the gift of new life, perhaps soon, perhaps at a time and place that is not yet known.

Job was shown the immensity of creation and that it was not all about him. There is a proper respect for vastness of the creation, and that this does not all revolve around humanity. At the same time humanity does matter to God. Psalm 8 speaks of the awesome nature of the heavens and the frailty of humanity in comparison; why should God notice such an insignificant creature? Yet the assertion is that, contrary to expectations, God does value humanity. Job, when raging at God, bitterly parodies that Psalm in Job 7:17: he would much rather *not* be noticed by God!

William Blake brings the psalmist's words back into its proper affirmative context when he places the words from Psalm 8 in the heavens above Job when he receives his vision of God in Plate 17.

R. S. Thomas struggled at times to believe that humanity is of worth to God, when viewed against the backdrop of the immensity of the universe and the aeons of time through which it has been evolving. His grasp on his own identity was tenuous: he called his autobiography 'Neb' which translated from the Welsh is 'no-one'. But Jason Walford Davies, who has translated the work, explains that this is somewhat more ambiguous than it would appear on the surface for "*neb*' in Welsh actually means 'someone'; it is in colloquial speech – or titles – when the word is cut adrift from syntax, that it has, incorrectly, the negative force of 'no-one'" (*Autobiographies*, 1997a: x).

This ambiguity of being no-one and someone R. S. Thomas expands on in the autobiography. He says:

gazing on the pre-Cambrian rocks in Braich y Pwll, R. S. realized that he was in contact with something that had been there for a thousand million years. His head would spin. A timescale such as this raised all kinds of questions and problems. On seeing his shadow fall on such ancient rocks, he had to question himself in a different context and ask the same old question as before, 'Who am I?', and the answer now came more emphatically than ever before, 'No-one.'

But a no-one with a crown of light about his head. He would remember a verse from Pindar: 'Man is a dream about a shadow. But when some splendour falls upon him from God, a glory comes to him and his life is sweet' (1997a: 78).

The psalmist, the writer of Job, William Blake, and R. S. Thomas all observe a reality which seems to speak of dissolution and re-formation, of insignificance and significance, of suffering and hope, of absence and presence, of disorientation and new orientation. To speak of only one part of the whole is not to be truthful. Neatly to rationalize the untidy realities of life sacrifices honesty on the altar of conceptual order. The poets of the Old Testament and the inheritors of those voices will not bow to these pressures. Are the unsettling issues still present in the story told in the New Testament?

Chapter Four
The unsettling death of Jesus

A. E. Dyson, speaking of R. S. Thomas's challenging poetry of the cross, says 'Such a vision is closer to Greek tragedy, to Hindu mythology, to agnostic doubt, even to atheism, than it is to middle-class churchgoing; it may well prove closer to the original New Testament documents, stripped of their deceptive familiarity, as well' (1990: 264).

Perhaps we have got used to seeing the New Testament story of Jesus' death as an inevitable happening. It had every appearance of being a tragic story but, if we approach it as a story of something that had to happen in order for humanity to be redeemed, then the tragedy is only apparent, for it was a necessary stage in God's plan. Our theoretical understanding of the meaning of the death shapes our perception of the event. Surely, we might think, in this most significant event for our Christian faith, God can have left nothing to chance and human reactions? Such a thought undermines our conception of God and his power. But as we have seen in our consideration of the Old Testament, faith can live with intense questioning, even questioning the character and purposes of God.

The historical/critical reading of the New Testament gospels strips away the 'deceptive familiarity'. This is a process where the documents as we have them now are recognized as being the story told by the early church of the life, death and resurrection of Jesus so that the hearers could know how to imitate the Christ in whom they believe (Burridge, 2007). If we want to know about the historical Jesus some very careful detective work has to be undertaken to get behind creative theological work of the gospel writers. The word 'creative' is not used here in a disparaging way or to imply that they just 'made it up', but is to recognize that theology is not done in a vacuum and that to tell of important events for a specific audience necessarily requires an element of interpretation.

The quest for the historical Jesus is a difficult one, and different conclusions can be reached. If, however, we believe that the man Jesus was perhaps the most significant historical figure of all time, a fascination with that figure seems highly appropriate. And because the world in which we live is very different to that of the first century, we may also want to interpret the historical data in a creative theological way for our times.

The scholar David Catchpole has spent a lifetime researching and reconstructing the life and words of the historical Jesus and when he comes to talk about the death of Jesus he makes it clear that there are two mindsets in the approach to that event that have a significant impact on how it is interpreted:

A clear logical distinction needs to be drawn between *intention* (thus: 'Jesus came into the world in order to die') and *result* (thus: 'Jesus died, but the aim of his mission was not to die but to call Israel to prepare for the inauguration of God's kingdom').
The *intention* scheme involves attaching meaning to a death *in advance*, which makes that death *theologically necessary*...
The *result* scheme, on the other hand, takes seriously a genuine sense of the tragic. It takes seriously the conflict that, with dispiriting normality, comes the way of the typical prophet, and it accepts that in one sense any such prophetic mission may end in 'failure'. But it does not see the ultimate outcome of the conflict or the 'failure' of the mission as inexorable or inevitable, and certainly not designed or desired...
Put another way: Jesus died, but the aim of his mission was not to die but to call Israel to prepare for the inauguration of God's kingdom (2006: 279,280,284).

It is not that Jesus' death in the *result* scheme has no significance – far from it. But the interpretation is applied retrospectively or when it becomes an inevitable event and there remains the possibility that things could have been very different. It shatters our idea that God will not let anything happen which is appallingly dreadful, unless that was his plan in some larger scheme. Humanity seems to have a freedom given by God that could take them to the abyss. Might it finally disappear into that abyss?

While there is no suggestion that R. S. Thomas was writing his poetry in response to such historical understandings as this, nevertheless such a viewpoint does raise questions about how God acts in the world, God's character, and of God's helplessness in the face of suffering imposed by humanity, issues very close to the heart of Thomas, which are intimately connected with his exploration of the cross. How do we talk of the faithfulness and presence of God in a world where the good, the supremely good, may suffer? How do we hold together the idea that morality and right behaviour are a correct response to God, and yet such behaviour may not appear to triumph, at least in the short term?

It was such dilemmas that drove the ancient Jews to conceptualize resurrection and it is therefore highly appropriate that the supremely good man, who yet died, was raised by God. But he did die and he did not come down from the cross, despite the taunts. So the resurrection does not answer the question about why the good should suffer, nor does it eliminate the tragedy of that death, but it does say that *in the end,* the intuition, the belief, that God will not allow evil to triumph, is vindicated. But what do we mean by 'in the end'?

The route to that final affirmation is not an easy one, and nor should it be. To refuse to acknowledge the pain of the world and the unresolved nature of the suffering that continues to haunt the planet, is to slip too easily into the Easter Sunday. We may think that we are doing the right thing in protecting God from harsh questioning, but the message of the psalms and of Job is that God does not condemn such language: far from it. Brueggemann puts it this way:

> Suspicion is not an academic act. It is an act of faith to enter into the suffering that gives the lie to theological triumphalism. In such a practice that does not need to protect God and does not fear to enter into the texts that voice protest, we may become more responsible Friday-Sunday people who know about truth and pain, about strength and weakness, about new life out of death. The canon insists upon such a horizon for faith. The God who hides in the canon knows about this horizon of life and is not scandalized by it (1999: 57).

As Job however discovered, attempting to put God on trial is not without risk, for not only is God put on trial, but more significantly perhaps, so is the questioner. For Job, eventually, a dialogue opened up and he began to see that, although he had a future with God; his God did speak to him and give him a value, nevertheless he had to acknowledge that there is a hiddenness about God, that there are things about which we have no knowledge and cannot speak.

Mark's gospel ends in chapter 16 with the empty tomb and the message from an angel to the women – that the empty place they see is where Jesus had been, but is no longer, for he is risen and will meet them in Galilee. In the original ending of Mark, that is how it finishes, with the women dazed by what they had seen and heard, confused as to the outcome, and not really comprehending the significance of what they had just witnessed. Entering into the mysterious presence can appropriately render one speechless.

There are things of which we cannot adequately speak and yet if we do not speak of them a potential is not realized for us or for others. The poet lives in this tension and gives a language that allows room for the unsaid to grow and expand. By not saying everything, but being suggestive and allusive, the poet comes to the points of experience and knowledge where it is important that we say something whilst at the same time recognizing the inadequacy of words. There are depths in the Crucifixion that are only plumbed by God and yet we know enough of these depths for it to be recognizable language with which to speak of suffering.

Resurrection is a hope and a belief founded on God, which has dimensions about it that we can only dimly and tentatively speculate. Yet it speaks of things we intuit in this life, too. It is in touching the universality of experience that crucifixion and resurrection takes on a mythic element. This is not to say that these events did not happen in history, for the foundation of the Christian faith is that a man named Jesus lived and died and rose again at a particular point in the history of the world, but the event also speaks of a reality that is known throughout history.

This is why we were able to speak of crucifixion and resurrection in the Old Testament and why the poet R. S. Thomas is able to speak of the cross not only as an event which occurred two thousand years ago, but as a universal experience and therefore appropriate language with which to describe the struggles of the remote Welsh hill farmer and his priest.

To talk of 'myth' raises rather similar issues we confronted when speaking of metaphor. There is an assumption that we are not talking about 'proper' truth, if truth at all, and that actually myth is a byword for something that is false. But myth, as Rowan Williams explains, is about 'the stories and symbols that lie so deep you can't work out who are the authors of them, the stories that give points of reference plotting your way in the inner and outer world' (2003: 5,6).

The idea is that myth gives you a way of talking about those events and happenings of life where there is a need to find some meaning beyond the surface interpretation, some way of indicating that yes, this happened in this time and this place, but it is also a part of a way of being that seems to be endlessly repeated. It does not explain those events, but it acknowledges that there is a bigger picture and that we need to find some relationship between our specific story and a more general pattern of being.

The cross may seem to be a specifically Christian story, but interestingly the Jewish artist Marc Chagall repeatedly painted the crucifixion, particularly in response to the persecution of the Jewish people by the Nazi regime. In his *The Creation of Man*, part of a series entitled *Message Biblique*, the crucifixion is depicted at the top of the painting. Chagall commented 'Ever since early childhood, I have been captivated by the Bible. It has always seemed to me, and still seems today, the greatest source of poetry of all time. Ever since then, I have searched for its reflection in life and in art. The Bible is like an echo of nature and this is the secret I have tried to convey... To my way of thinking, these paintings do not illustrate the dream of a single people, but that of mankind' (quoted in *Chagall*, Jacob Baal-Teshuva, 2008: 207).

The New Testament story of Jesus' death, when removed from explanatory atonement theory, seems as profoundly unsettling as any of the stories in the Old Testament. Far from ironing out the wrinkles in the fabric of our understanding, the death of Jesus draws us into a world where the reason is torn. Rowan Williams, in his book *Christ on Trial*, speaks of the gospel writer Mark's depiction of the trial of Jesus. This is a world where the sentence has been decided prior to the trial: 'He is going to die, because that is what the world has decided' (2000:7). The powerlessness of Jesus before his judges overturns our judgement of what God is or should be like. The story demands of us that we re-examine our ideas about God:

> Mark is inviting us to think again about what we mean by transcendence. Normally, when we use such words, we think of God's surpassing greatness, but how can we avoid that becoming simply a massive projection of what *we* mean by greatness? . . . If we are really to have our language about the transcendence – the sheer, unimaginable *differentness* – of God recreated, it must be by emptying out of all we thought we knew about it, the emptying out of practically all we normally mean by greatness. No more about the lofty distance of God, *the sovereignty that involves control over all the circumstances* (2000: 7) (my emphasis).

The psalmists and Job had to go through a period of disorientation, of leaving behind a stable, ordered world where the good are inevitably rewarded with untold blessings. This is not an easy movement but honesty demands that of us. The gospel story still makes those same demands. But there is also, in the gospel story, the hope of resurrection, but the move to new orientation is not necessarily an easy transition, one which arises solely out of determined effort: it is born of grace.

Being a follower of Jesus, a disciple, cannot bypass the difficulties of life. There has to be a willingness to let go of that which is held most dear, even life itself, and paradoxically that is the very way to life. Jesus says, 'Whoever wants to save his life will lose it, but whoever loses his life for my sake and for the gospel's will save it' (Mark 8: 35).

Paul also spoke of the need to enter into dispossession, to identify with Christ in his death in order to enter into resurrection experience. This movement is not a once for all event, but a continuous cycle: 'My one desire is to know Christ and the power of his resurrection, and to share his sufferings in growing conformity with his death, in hope of somehow attaining the resurrection of the dead. It is not that I have already achieved this. I have not yet reached perfection, but I press on, hoping to take hold of that for which Christ once took hold of me' (Philippians 3: 10,11). For Paul, resurrection had a future aspect, but it also had a reality in this life.

If we speak of a life being 'saved', what do we mean? Perhaps there have been times when salvation language has referred more to the future than the present but the biblical witness is that we need to think of the implications of salvation for this life. There is both a 'now' and a 'not yet' element to resurrection experience. The death of Jesus has always had this interpretive link with a life that is 'saved' but perhaps it is more helpful to think of this in terms of a life that becomes willing to enter into the disorientation of death that Christ experienced in order to move by grace to the new orientation of resurrection. This is about relationship rather than intellectual understanding. By becoming conformed to God in Christ, we are pulled in the direction of God's way of being in the world. This may not be a comfortable experience because it may run against the grain of our own will or that of the world.

When the BBC screened an adaptation of the novel *Jane Eyre* by Charlotte Brontë in 2006, the actor Toby Stephens, who plays Rochester, was interviewed by Christopher Middleton:

"When Jane first comes into his life, he's stern and morose because he's used to leading this solitary life," says Stephens (Rochester was duped into marrying the deranged but beautiful Bertha). "Gradually, though, Jane releases him from his past, saves him, becomes his moral compass, till in the end, they're not just friends, they're soulmates" (2006: 14).

Stephens defines the salvation that Jane offers to Rochester as being a release from his past and a fresh moral orientation grounded in his relationship with her. Salvation, in the sense of rescuing someone from themselves and from destructive forces, is still a term used in common parlance. We cannot be sure of what happens to us beyond this life, but to believe in a God who wills to life, is to orientate oneself in a particular direction. This may result, paradoxically, in suffering, in a sort of death, not only for oneself but also on behalf of another.

Rochester eventually entered into life maimed but whole, having risked his life in trying to save his first wife. Jane suffered intensely in refusing to fall in with Rochester's plans of living together as an unmarried couple (once the bigamous wedding preparations were exposed for what they were) and entered a wilderness experience both metaphorically and literally as a result, but her steadfastness was eventually rewarded. But the actions of risk, privation and suffering were not taken in order to reap the reward; they were taken for their own sake.

R. S. Thomas was consistently diffident about saying whether there would be a life for him beyond this one:

> In the face of all this, in the end, the only attitude for a wise man is humility. What mortal can say how it was before the existence of the world, or how it will be after it has ceased to exist according to the second law of thermodynamics? R.S. is no-one. He leaves it to God to decide whether he will become someone in another world; whether there is work for him to do in some mysterious future, or whether he is a link between here and some other kind of existence. (*Autobiographies*, 1997a: 105)

Thomas explored these issues further in his talk '*Where Do We Go From Here*' (*Selected Prose*, 1995b: 120,121):

> There is no God but God. The very use of the word answers all questions. The ability to create life automatically posits the ability to re-create it... I must end this talk, surely, by telling you how he has revealed himself to me, if that is the right way to describe the knowledge – half hope, half intuition – by which I live.

"'When the sun rises, do you not see a round disc of fire somewhat like a guinea?' Oh no no, I see an innumerable company of the heavenly host crying, 'Holy, Holy, Holy is the Lord God Almighty!' I question not my corporeal or vegetative eye any more than I would question a window concerning sight. I look through it and not with it." So said William Blake, and, similarly, in my humbler way, say I.... May it not be that alongside us, made invisible by the thinnest of veils, is the heaven we seek? The immortality we must put on? ... To a country man it is the small field suddenly lit up by a ray of sunlight. It is T. S. Eliot's "still point, there the dance is", Wordsworth's "central peace, subsisting at the heart of endless agitation". It is even closer. It is within us, as Jesus said. That is why there is no need to go anywhere from here.

Salvation is an orientation towards that which is good, to God. But this may entail suffering borne individually and for another. In losing life, life might be gained. This is not to glorify suffering or to have a theory of the necessity of suffering: it is simply an observation that this seems often to be the way of this world. Barack Obama noticed this when he met, over a period of time, with black Christian ministers in Chicago. They were open to him and told him their stories:

One minister talked about a former gambling addiction. Another told me about his years as a successful executive and a secret drunk. They all mentioned periods of religious doubt; the corruption of the world and their own hearts; the striking bottom and shattering of pride; and then finally the resurrection of self, a self alloyed to something larger. That was the source of their confidence, they insisted; their personal fall, their subsequent redemption. It was what gave them authority to preach the Good News (2007: 279,280).

Similarly this was the experience of Jacques Pohier who was banned in 1979 by the Vatican from preaching, celebrating the Eucharist and teaching. *God in Fragments* (1985) is his autobiographical work of theology as he sought to live through the experience of disorientation and see if anything emerged on the other side. 'Decomposition' was the word that haunted him 'not in the biological sense of rotting away, but as an indication of the way in which one has to dismantle the various elements of an inlaid surface in order to put them together again in a new order, since the old world has gone' (1985: 3). This was a profoundly destabilizing experience affecting him not primarily at an intellectual level, but in the depths of his being (1985: 60). He came to the conclusion that unless he let go of what he thought he knew of God, then he would not be able to come through to a place of new understanding. 'I had to let him be himself, let him go, so that he would return as he wanted, when he wanted, in the way he wanted. I had to renounce God' (1985: 69). He recognized that we can only know in part – that is, know God in fragments:

> The resurrection of Jesus Christ and the Pentecost of his Spirit do not mean that Jesus Christ is henceforward the answer to everything ('Jesus or nothing') and that in him Christians from now on have the answer to everything. They indicate that God bears witness that the question raised by Jesus Christ is the one by which God manifests himself, that the reply given by God in Jesus Christ is what human beings can expect of God (1985: 294).

So how do we communicate the partial knowledge that we have? We can tell stories and write poems of the experience of moving from the place where we thought we knew, through the dismantling of that knowledge, to an experiment with a new language of God which does not claim to be a totalizing experience that excludes all other speech, but is what has been given to us for now. It is some comfort to realize that many others have travelled this same road of loss and recovery, but recovery to a place of greater maturity.

The poet/priest George Herbert pictured this dynamic in his poem 'Easter Wings'. He literally pictured it, for it is a pattern poem and the words and lines form the shape of angel wings. At the narrowest point of the two stanzas he becomes firstly 'Most poor:' and secondly 'Most thin.' But, at the narrowest point, the eye takes in the next line, and observes that God is also at the thinnest point for it reads, 'With thee' and thus the start of the ascent upwards comes from God, and it transpires that, 'Affliction shall advance the flight in me'.

So, over these four chapters, we have seen that there is a need to find a way of talking of the death and resurrection of Christ in a way that moves beyond theory. Stories, poetry, art are such ways that leave room for the interpretation of the one who reads and sees. They touch people at a level other than simply rational analysis, which is not to decry the need for analytical thought, but it is not everything. Inherited theological beliefs can be undermined by the observation of the world as it is and we saw that unsettling movement in the Old Testament witness in the Psalms and Job.

But the coming of Christ has not eliminated the challenges to faith, for his death raises the same problems of suffering and the implications for the character of God. For faith to be authentic, voices need to be raised in examining the questions from various perspectives, in the way that the pursuit of truth in a courtroom is advanced by hearing the voices of more than one witness. The Jewish witnesses were not afraid to do this, to realize this is part of the dialogue of a faith community. The path from the known may lead through a time of disorientation. But the pattern of movement through disorientation to a new orientation, given as a gift of God, seems to be the experience of many. To talk of this experience as crucifixion and resurrection gives us a language which links this dynamic to the foundational event of the Christian faith, but it also links it to a universal, mythic, experience.

We turn now to the poetry of R. S. Thomas, the inheritor of the biblical voice of counter-testimony, who unflinchingly explores over his long life the difficulties, the doubts, and the absence of God, often using language of the cross with which to do this. He also enters however into the hope of resurrection as experienced as a foretaste in this life, particularly through his appreciation of the Welsh people, landscapes and seascapes – although this is always an ambiguous matter. The mind and the heart are in tension as he pursues these themes but he tenaciously holds to his task and out of this comes the most moving poetry that takes the reader on a journey which will not be satisfied with a superficial resolution but enables continuing 'exploration into God' (to use a phrase popularized by Bishop John A. T. Robinson).

Chapter Five
The shock of Wales

Ronald Thomas (he added the Stuart later) was born in 1913 in Cardiff. His father was a sailor. This required the family to move around in Thomas's early years, but in 1918 they settled in Holyhead, Anglesey. He was an only child and despite having Welsh parents was brought up in an anglicized way and did not learn Welsh until he was in his thirties. As his father was often away at sea, much of the child rearing fell to his mother and she had a great love of the countryside and imparted this love to her son. But there was a complexity in the relationship between mother and son and R. S. Thomas found her to be too possessive and suffocating and when the time came for him to go to the University at Bangor he did so with alacrity, seeing it as an escape. After training for the priesthood in Llandaff, he went to his first curacy in Chirk on the Welsh/English borders and there he met and married his English wife, the painter Mildred (Elsi) Eldridge.

But the realities of life there started to impact on the inexperienced young curate. R. S. Thomas reports in his autobiography *Neb,* 'It was here, for the first time, that he came face to face with the problem of pain. Some of the parishioners were very ill and required frequent visiting ... The curate was more than eager to help these people, but how? Slowly, by reading and thinking, he came to understand that this was one of the greatest problems to have troubled man since he started using his brain' (*Autobiographies,*1997a: 43).

After a second curacy, in Hanmer, he was appointed rector of Manafon in Mid Wales. Years later, reflecting back on those early experiences as a rector, he told John Ormond, in the TV documentary on the poet, that

> I was brought up hard against this community and I really began to learn what human nature, rural human nature was like. And I must say that I found nothing that I'd been told or taught in theological college was of any help at all in these circumstances. It was just up to me to find my own way amongst these people.
>
> Well, I came out of a kind of bourgeois environment which, especially in modern times, is protected; it's cushioned from some of the harsher realities, and this muck and blood and hardness, the rain and the spittle and the phlegm of farm life was, of course, a

shock to begin with and one felt that this was something not quite part of the order of things. But, as one experienced it and saw how definitely part of their lives this was, sympathy grew in oneself and compassion and admiration (1972b: 49,50).

It was in confronting this world, an alien one to him, that provoked him into poetry. It was his movement from comfortable orientation into disorientation. R. S. Thomas tells how

On a dark, cold day in November, on his way to visit a family in a farm over a thousand feet above sea-level, he saw the farmer's brother out in the field, docking mangels. The thing made a profound impression on him, and when he returned to the house after the visit he set about writing 'A Peasant', the first poem to attempt to face the reality of the scenes around him. (1997a: 52)

This was a turning point for R. S. Thomas, a seminal moment. He had written poetry before, but not like this, and the experiences of his early life as a priest stripped away escapism. As an old man he retells, in the South Bank TV documentary, that moment of observation, of vision. It was so real, he says, emphasizing the word 'real' (1991).

To the 'peasant' he gave the name 'Iago Prytherch' and he was to become an archetypal figure who frequented Thomas's poems for many years:

That man, Prytherch, with the torn cap,
I saw him often, framed in the gap
Between two hazels with his sharp eyes,
Bright as thorns, watching the sunrise
Filling the valley with its pale yellow
Light, where the sheep and the lambs went haloed
With grey mist lifting from the dew...
                        For he's still there
At early morning, when the light is right
And I look up suddenly at a bird's flight.
(1955, 'The Gap in the Hedge': 53)

J. P. Ward comments that this might be suggestive of a crucifixion scene. 'The peasant is "between two hazels", perhaps thieves crucified, and a crown of "thorns" can at least enter into our consciousness. At the end of the poem ... there is, equally a touch of suggestion of Easter morning' (1987: 19).

This poem captures so many of the words and features with which we will become familiar in Thomas's poetry. There is the gap, the sunrise and the half-light, the natural world, the lamb, the birds, the visual awareness, the word 'torn'. It can work at the level of description of this imaginary yet real figure from the Welsh rural farming community, but it also has that suggestion that life is held between the torn nature of a thorny crucifixion and the early resurrection morning, if we only know how to look.

The early poems of R. S. Thomas mostly concentrate on Wales but the religious themes are there from the start. There is a dynamic of crucifixion and resurrection giving shape to his reflections on the reality he found in the harsh landscape and peasant community of rural Wales. As he stressed, he had seen something real. Is it possible that the reality he speaks of is not just the reality of that part of Wales but also a reality undergirding the rhythm of life and death?

R. S. Thomas never pretended to be an easy 'man of the people'. As a gauche young priest his work had taken him beyond the familiar and comfortable culture in which he had been brought up and challenged him with a completely different way of life, where suffering and privation were close to the surface. He did not find this easy, either at an intellectual level or at the level of relationships. But he was grateful for the shock that tipped him over into a new world of perception, thought, feeling and poetry. Later he would speak of his debt to 'Prytherch, the man / Who more than all directed my slow /Charity where there was need.' From what he had seen, he was able to tell in poetry

    . . . the story of one whose hands
    Have bruised themselves on the locked doors
    Of life; whose heart, fuller than mine
    Of gulped tears, is the dark well
    From which to draw, drop after drop,
    The terrible poetry of his kind. (1961a, 'The Dark Well': 9).

Did Prytherch become, at some level, and on some occasions, Christ to him? Thomas could speak of the rural peasant in sometimes harsh and uncomprehending language, but he recognized that the figure had opened up a gap in his understanding and that in that gap he could catch a glimpse, when the light was right, of somebody who knew a greater depth of sorrow than he could ever know, and from that greater depth of reality he could now draw his poetry. It was a terrible poetry but it could also take flight and wing its way heavenwards, so introducing us to the idea that the figure in the gap, although seen as the crucified one, can also, simultaneously, lift the heart with a lightness that is beyond understanding.

Gaps and silence, the space where God is both found and yet not comprehended, resonates with the Old Testament record of the mercy seat above the Ark of the Covenant, the space which is framed by two golden cherubim (Exodus Ch 25). Rowan Williams, in his sermon 'Holy Space', refers to this 'gap': 'In our history, the only possibility of knowing God as God is to face the silence, at least sometimes, the absence between the cherubim; only by doing so can we learn to look to a God who is free to forgive and re-create because he is not bound by our imaginings. ... It is in the life and death of the Lamb of God that the silence culminates; it is in his life and death that we know there is no more need for a mercy seat, and the veil of the sanctuary is torn down. ... And at last, a silence not between the cherubim but between two thieves, and an absence between two white-clad figures in a burial vault' (1994: 101,102,103). The silence comes to its greatest intensity in the Lamb, yet, paradoxically, it is a silence that 'speaks' to the heart. It is real.

But R. S. Thomas was aware that the peasant could not find the words to articulate what the heart knew. In a longer than normal poem for him, Thomas tells the story in 'The Airy Tomb' (1955: 37-41) of Twm who was a failure at school but came into his own when released back into his familiar hill farming environment. However, the pattern of his days was tragically interrupted by the death of his father, followed before the year was out, by the death of his mother. Unable to articulate his grief, he got on with the farm work but he

Was aware of something for which he had no name,
Though the one tree, which dripped through the winter
    night
With a clock's constancy, tried hard to tell
The insensitive mind what the heart knew well.

But March led into April, and

On Easter Day he heard the first warbler sing

In the quick ash by the door, and the snow made room
On the sharp turf for the first fumbling lamb.

We have here imagery that becomes familiar to us: there is 'the one tree' which resonates with the tree of the cross; the drips of the rain, which echo with the drips of blood; and the landscape expressing the dark night of crucifixion, communicating what is felt deeply yet the mind cannot quite grasp.

But April is also the month redolent of resurrection. Thomas remarks in *A Year in Llŷn* that 'In the West the month [April] is heavily influenced by Christianity with its message of the victory over death, prompted by the return of life to the withered and barren earth' (*Autobiographies*, 1997a: 132).

So the association of Easter Day in April with the first hearing of the bird in the tree, the sight of new grass and the lamb: these carry the message of resurrection and victory of some sort. However with R. S. Thomas the joy is never unambiguous, and, as Brueggemann suggests with the experience of new orientation, the memory of the disorientation is still present. There is a cutting edge to Thomas's observations, for it is a 'quick' ash, the turf is 'sharp', we remember the chill of the snow, and the lamb is 'fumbling'. And the conclusion of the poem is no happy ending, for Twm continues his solitary life and dies a solitary death 'entombed in the lucid weather' and it is a fortnight before his body is found. Theories of atonement that speak of victory have this claim challenged by the ongoing sorrow, suffering and death.

There is no easy, automatic, progression from darkness to light from crucifixion to resurrection. In Thomas's poem 'The Minister', a narrative for four voices, broadcast by the BBC in 1953, the narrator says (1955: 81),

But for some there is no dawn, only the light
Of the Cross burning up the long aisle
Of night; and for some there is not even that.

'The Minister', R. S. Thomas made clear, was not autobiographical for it was a non-conformist minister of the Welsh chapel who came as an idealistic youngster to the Welsh hill community, only to be tamed and destroyed by the worldly wise diaconate. But there are occasions when Thomas seems to be speaking out of his own experience. The Minister says

They listened to me preaching the unique gospel
Of love; but our eyes never met. And outside
The blood of God darkened the evening sky. (1955: 91,92)

In *Neb* Thomas says of those early years as a rector at Manafon, 'Meanwhile he had to learn the craft of being a young rector amongst rough and hardened farmers who expected more from him than he could give; while they in turn failed to meet his own ideals' (1997a: 51). R. S. Thomas had his own move from orientation through to disorientation. He went through his own sort of crucifixion experience in facing the suffering and hardship amongst his parishioners and in finding that what he offered in terms of the gospel fell to the floor between them.

His theological training may have suggested to him that he would have the answers to bring to his parishioners. But the reality of life undermined these certainties. As with Blake's Job, he moved from a theoretical knowledge to confrontation with a world that simply did not conform to neat hypotheses. And he begins to protest. But it seemed to him that the swelling sense of protest at the harshness of life is sometimes stifled by a God who overwhelms. As the priest views the suffering Davies who is ill in both mind and body, yet labours unremittingly on, the priest is silenced by divine fiat:

And so you work
In the wet fields and suffer pain
And loneliness as a tree takes
The night's darkness, the day's rain;
While I watch you, and pray for you,
And so increase my small store
Of credit in the bank of God,
Who sees you suffer and me pray
And touches you with the sun's ray,
That heals not, yet blinds my eyes
And seals my lips as Job's were sealed
Imperiously in the old days. (1955, 'Priest and Peasant': 109)

This is not the Job who is reconciled to his Maker but a Job who finds God to be distant and apparently unmoved in the face of the suffering. It is a God who sees but silences. Moreover this God is not only unmoved but appears to be culpable in creating a world where he is implicated in creating both beauty and suffering:

Who said to the trout,
You shall die on Good Friday
To be food for a man
And his pretty lady?

It was I, said God,
Who formed the roses
In the delicate flesh
And the tooth that bruises. (1955, 'Pisces': 110)

And yet the next to last poem in the volume *Song at the Year's Turning* is the significant 'In a Country Church' (1955: 114). The silence here is not only of the priest, but of God. Except in the silence there comes a visionary experience, a transformation of the blinding light:

To one kneeling down no word came, ...

Was he balked by silence? He kneeled long,
And saw love in a dark crown
Of thorns blazing, and a winter tree
Golden with fruit of a man's body.

Here is the poet's ability to hold opposites together, so that the crucifixion and resurrection merge into one. Winter and summer come together. The opposite perspectives of Hopewell's church stories are married in a way that prose is unable to do, that theory is unable to express. Here the God is no longer on the outside, but is seen in the man's body, an embodied love, darkly suffering yet radiant with promise and light.

R. S. Thomas is sometimes criticized for his lack of Christian love and compassion and is felt to have a greater affinity with the God of the Old Testament (with the highly questionable implication that the Old Testament God is quite different from the one of the New Testament). Thomas was hesitant in using the word 'love' of God, believing that we domesticate God too freely. However there are some notable occasions when the word 'love', or the compassionate regard that lies behind that word, find its way into his poetry – and it becomes all the more significant for not having been used in a profligate way.

We become aware of the importance of reading R. S. Thomas as a whole. His individual poems play against each other and the totality brings a richness and a challenge that concentration on one poem alone, however rewarding, cannot bring. One moment we are reading of a God who is outside of our experience, who appears not to care but uses his power to silence protest, who creates a world both of beauty and of suffering, and then we see a God who speaks no words of consolation or explanation but is there in love, in Christ (for the reference is to the crucifixion) and that somehow the suffering is productive of fruit.

R. S. Thomas is a highly visual poet, and light is a key component in his artistry. In his interview with Lethbridge, Thomas comments, 'What I have tried to say is that when the sunlight comes through the window and dances on the floor, is not that one of God's means of trying to get in contact with me?' (1983b: 55). Light is one of the ways God 'speaks' for Thomas, although it is not unambiguous as the light can blind also. The absence of light, the illuminating light and the excess of light, speak with an emotional, intuitive impact, taking the reader imaginatively into the darkness of crucifixion and the light of resurrection and the awesome light of a mysterious God.

The landscape photographer Joe Cornish says: 'First, light. Everything else follows, for light is the language of photography as well as its raw material. As a poet uses words, so a photographer uses light... If we 'feel' light, our pictures will touch hearts, have an emotional impact... Light is a universal language with depths and nuances I am still learning' (2002: 11). But perhaps the poet uses light also and utilizes that emotional depth and universal language as a means of communicating truths about this world and God.

R. S. Thomas can look out over the landscape, which to him is the created world, and see it as something in process. Yet paradoxically it is also something which is complete. The dynamic of darkness and light, crucifixion and resurrection, are continually at play:

Then there is movement,
Change, as slowly the cloud bruises
Are healed by sunlight, or snow caps
A black mood; but gold at evening
To cheer the heart. All through history
The great brush has not rested,
Nor the paint dried; yet what eye,

Looking coolly, or, as we now,
Through the tears' lenses, ever saw
This work and it was not finished? (1958, 'The View from the
Window': 27)

If R. S. Thomas felt the limits of the consolation he could bring through
words to his flock, then somehow the deep mysteries of the Eucharistic
bread and wine might yet speak. They certainly were a consolation and
a source of spiritual nourishment to Thomas himself:

Hunger was loneliness, betrayed
By the pitiless candour of the stars'
Talk, in an old byre he prayed

.   .   .   .

He prayed for love, love that would share
His rags' secret; rising he broke
Like sun crumbling the gold air

The live bread for the starved folk. (1958, 'Bread': 46)

The line ending suggests, momentarily, that there is a brokenness in
R. S. Thomas as he ceremonially 'breaks bread' for the people who are
hungry yet may not know their need. But the brokenness is transfigured
by the light into something greater than he could understand.

Brokenness, being torn, appears to be part of the life with God and in
God. And no satisfactory theoretical explanation seems to fully answer
the question of why this should be. This is not to suggest that Thomas is
uninterested in understanding with the mind, for he devoted a lifetime to
studying, reading, thinking, trying to discern a reason, but he never found
a solution with which reason could be finally satisfied.

His book *Tares* takes its title from the parable of the Wheat and the
Tares: 'Didst not thou sow good seed in the field? From whence, then,
hath it tares?' Matt 13:27. This is exactly the problem. Is it the work of
an enemy, as the parable suggests, or is that too simple a solution, when
fundamental to God's creation seems to be both wheat and tares? The
punning quality of the word suggests that tears as in rending, and tears as
in weeping, are intrinsic to the world.

Yet the tears can be transformative and beautiful for Thomas tells of
a powerful memory he had of watching Kreisler play, when the poet was
so close he could see the physical strain of making the music:

This player who so beautifully suffered
For each of us upon his instrument.

So it must have been on Calvary
In the fiercer light of the thorns' halo: ...
Because it was himself that he played
And closer than all of them the God listened.   (1961a, 'The
Musician': 19)

There is no explanation here, but somehow the suffering of Christ
on Calvary has created a music that is redemptive. It is a perplexing,
contradictory music, for it is a melody that unsettles as well as soothes.

In the powerful poem 'Here' (1961a: 43) the opening line is 'I am a
man now.' Is this the child or humanity grown up, or is it in fact a poem
about Christ, as Dyson suggests? (1990: 263). It does indeed seem that
humanity grown up, evolved, comes to fruition in a man who says

I am like a tree,
From my top boughs I can see
The footprints that led up to me.

There is blood in my veins
That has run clear of the stain
Contracted in so many loins.

At the head of the evolutionary tree is an innocent man hanging on a
tree. 'Why?' cries this man:

Why, then, are my hands red
With the blood of so many dead?
Is this where I was misled?

Why are my hands this way
That they will not do as I say?
Does no God hear when I pray?

We have echoes here of the cry of dereliction from the cross, using the
words from Psalm 22. But although this is Christ, the allusive language

also allows this to be interpreted as the cry of humanity – Christ is the representative man 'here'.

And for all those who say that R. S. Thomas is not a man of compassionate sensitivity, of Christian grace, the last stanza belies this for it seems to bring such tenderness to the depiction of Christ on the cross:

It is too late to start
For destinations not of the heart.
I must stay here with my hurt.

It might have been sensible, at head level so to speak, for God to set off for some other destination, but such possibilities are 'too late'; for what is done is done. The destination, the hanging on the tree, is one of the heart, not the mind. There is to be no abandonment of that destination, for God, God in Christ the man, must stay 'here', along with his hurt, even if this is a place of silence and, paradoxically, abandonment. This 'hurt' is not only his own pain but refers to humanity who are the 'hurt' of God.

Dyson says of this poem:

Is there something *in* the Cross ... which by its actual nature bypasses theology and, at the level of language and image, testifies to itself? 'I am a man now': the image of evolved man, alone in a creation where God is dead, is held in exact silhouette against the other image of Christ on the Cross, when God is absent. If the Christian religion has this paradox at its heart, perhaps it is not irrelevant to modern doubt after all, but simply an anticipation of it by 2000 years. And, if the revelation of love is 'Here', where the title directs us, then Christian faith and love have perhaps always been odder than naïve belief, or unbelief, would like us to suppose (1990: 263,264).

In the collection of poems *Pietà* there continues that sense of movement through disorientation to newness. The costliness of the exploration is evident. In his search for truth, 'for the door to myself', the poet has to 'overdraw on my balance / Of air' and plunge into the watery depths, perhaps resonating with the baptismal depths of dying with Christ. In losing his life, he will find it (cf. Mark 8:35):

I must go down with the poor
Purse of my body and buy courage,
Paying for it with the coins of my breath.' (1966, 'This To Do':
12)

The cross is still central. In the title poem he observes

And in the foreground
The tall Cross,
Sombre, untenanted,
Aches for the Body
That is back in the cradle
Of a maid's arms. (1966, *Pietà*: 14)

Why does the Cross ache? Is it in sympathy, or does it ache for the
crucifixion to continue? The Cross is untenanted, a word recurring in
the poem 'In Church' (1966: 44), where Thomas is left alone in a church
following the service, when the silence re-invades the building:

There is no other sound
In the darkness but the sound of a man
Breathing, testing his faith
On emptiness, nailing his questions
One by one to an untenanted cross.

As Christ has been nailed to the cross, does the crucifixion continue
in some sense with the priest who battles to find some answers to the
suffering that the cross represents? Or is it a fruitless task because of
the emptiness, the sense of absence? Is the empty cross a negative or a
positive symbol? Does emptiness betoken God's absence or is it empty
because the suffering is over, the man is back in the arms of one who
humanly loves him, and will be raised to life within the loving arms of
God? The testing of faith is not necessarily a negative thing; the testing
of Job's faith led him to abandon the wrong certainties he had previously
lived by in order to find a different sort of God, not a God he could
necessarily understand, but still a God with whom he could have an
ongoing relationship.

And there are moments for R. S. Thomas when answers of a sort
come, and the promise of resurrection is experienced. One such moment

is in 'The Moor' (1966: 24). Here there is a silence also, but now it is not symbolic of God's absence, nor is it an imperiously imposed silence. Words are not the way the communication happens, questions and answers are simply not relevant. 'What God was there made himself felt, / Not listened to, in clean colours':

> There were no prayers said. But stillness
> Of the heart's passions – that was praise
> Enough; and the mind's cession
> Of its kingdom. I walked on,
> Simple and poor, while the air crumbled
> And broke on me generously as bread.

R. S. Thomas does not talk conventionally in his poetry of repentance and forgiveness. But here we have a sort of repentance, in terms of a new orientation, but expressed in different words. There is a yielding of his mind and its rights to self-government, a quieting of the turbulent emotions and strongly felt passions, leaving him free, uncomplicated and unburdened to walk on with a light step. There is an overwhelming generosity in the air reviving him, resonating with the manna-like bread of the Eucharist, giving absolution.

It is a moment of unfettered joy in the life of the priest who had found that being a rector is not an easy spiritual journey. He had tried to minister to the sick and ill parishioners, visiting them frequently, bringing what comforts he was able: 'I read him the psalms, / Said prayers and was still.' But it seems to the priest to be a thin sort of comfort and the harsh realities of parish life grind him down:

> Nine years in that bed
> From season to season
> The great frame rotted,
> While the past's slow stream,
> Flowing through his head,
> Kept the rusty mill
> Of the mind turning–
> It was I it ground. (1963a, 'The Mill': 40)

And it was not only the suffering of those who were ill that caused Thomas to fall from the easy idealism of his youthful curacy. There is a mutual disappointment when priest and people come together for worship:

> We stand looking at
> Each other. I take the word 'prayer'
> And present it to them. I wait idly,
> Wondering what their lips will
> Make of it. But they hand back
> Such presents. I am left alone
> With no echoes to the amen
> I dreamed of. (1966, 'Service': 36)

The easy early orientation of the psalmist and of Job for whom belief in God, at that stage, is straightforward has led on to the disorientation when life impinges on them. The disappointments, the suffering in the world, the rejection by others and the absence of God are their own crucifixion. The suffering of God in Christ on the cross gives shape to the reflections, but it is not an explanation but a further illustration of the problem. However the movement to disorientation is followed, not once and for all, but in a cyclical way, with moments of joy and resurrection promise. The sadness and the salvation are superimposed on each other; there is no way back to the early orientation, but a new way of being is sometimes possible for the older and wiser poet/priest.

But the 'No' of life, the title of a poem in *Not that he Brought Flowers*, the last collection of poems at which we will look in this chapter, results in poetry:

> So the Thing came
> Nearer him, and its breath caused
> Him to retch, and none knew why.
> But he rested for one long month,
> And after began to sing
> For gladness, and the Thing stood,
> Letting him, for a year, for two;
> Then put out its raw hand
> And touched him, and the wound took
> Over, and the nurses wiped off
> The poetry from his cracked lips. (1968, 'No': 10)

Some may see the poet as a 'crippled soul ... limping through life / On his prayers'. He has not chosen, or been chosen for, the easy option:

> 'There are other people
> In the world, sitting at table
> Contented, though the broken body
> And the shed blood are not on the menu'.

'Let it be so', I say, 'Amen and amen'. (1968, 'The Priest': 29)

There is an acceptance here of the sacrificial life, a recognition that a comfortable life can be had without imbibing the desolation of life that the Eucharist represents, but the spiritual price to be paid is too high. Some may choose the comfortable life, but the priest will go the way of the cross, even if it means going up the 'green lane' in gladness and coming down in the dark, 'feeling the cross warp / In his hands'.

Words are the way the poet communicates, but the experience (perhaps the experience and the silence are one and the same?) is primary. These are moments to savour, to hold that space for a moment, to wait, because the communication can never quite match that reality. This is our problem: to speak of the Real, as we must if we want to communicate the experience to others, but to recognize that our words are inadequate:

> Moments of great calm,
> Kneeling before an altar
> Of wood in a stone church
> In summer, waiting for the God
> To speak; ...
> Prompt me, God;
> But not yet. When I speak,
> Though it be you who speak
> Through me, something is lost.
> The meaning is in the waiting. (1968, 'Kneeling': 32)

Chapter Six
Experimentation

R. S. Thomas moved West in 1954 from Manafon to Eglwys Fach – near to the sea, on the main road to Aberystwyth. Although, as a young man, he had been happy to escape from Holyhead, as time passed he became assailed by this great longing, yearning, *hiraeth*, for the mountains and sea to the West. The surrounding hill country of Manafon assuaged to some extent the desire for something other than the flat landscape of his curacy in Hanmer, but there was still that longing for the sea that overwhelmed him. There was also the desire to be in Welsh speaking Wales, now that he had learnt Welsh.

So the move to Eglwys Fach seemed to be taking him in the right direction, but unknown to him, the area was popular with the English. R. S. Thomas was passionate about Wales, its heritage, landscape and its future. Particularly he believed that the Welsh people had sold out to the English; Welsh identity was disappearing fast and a highly significant cause and symptom of this was the erosion of the Welsh language. He wanted a Welsh Wales for the future.

R. S. Thomas had to struggle in his own life to find his Welsh identity. Although he was Welsh, he had been brought up to be English in speech and outlook. In his adult life he sought to reclaim that Welsh heritage for himself, and the learning of the Welsh language was an important part of that. But he could never write poetry in Welsh to the standards he demanded of himself (although he did write prose in Welsh). This was a cause of great grief to him. But the creative artist in him would not allow for compromise in this area.

Eglwys Fach proved to be a disappointment for Thomas. The experiences of Manafon lived in him whilst he was at Eglwys Fach and helped in the inspiration of his poetry but he was starting to run out of inspiration. In 1967 the opportunity came for him to move to Aberdaron on the Llŷn Peninsula. At last he could be in Welsh-speaking Wales with the sea literally on his doorstep (the church is almost on the beach), not far from Anglesey.

The move to Aberdaron had something of the feeling of coming home and this had implications for his poetry. R. S. Thomas writes of 'finding himself in a totally Welsh community in Aberdaron, he no longer felt it necessary to emphasize his Welshness, only to accept it as a completely natural fact. Welsh was the language of the majority of the inhabitants, and there was no question of anything else in their homes or in their meetings. He had reached the destination of his own personal pilgrimage' (1997a: 77). What therefore to write about?

> Having reached Aberdaron, however, not only was there no *hiraeth* for Eglwys-fach – it wasn't the source of many poems, either. To tell the truth, his muse had dried up. Having kept on writing for a quarter of a century about the life of the countryside, and later about the condition of Wales, he had milked the subject pretty dry, and it was fortunate that he changed publishers with his next book ... He therefore turned to Macmillan with his new book, a book that displayed new subject-matter and a new style... he turned increasingly to the question of the soul, the nature and existence of God, and the problem of time in the universe. (1997a: 73,76)

As we have seen, the religious themes were there from the start of his poetry, but these were interwoven with meditation on the identity of the Welsh hill farmer and the Welsh landscape and the future of Wales. Now the earlier religious themes are distilled into a more intense experimentation with the ways of speaking and thinking about God.

Richard Harries quotes from a 1981 BBC Radio 4 interview with R. S. Thomas in which he said 'God has given the answer to suffering in the Incarnation and the Crucifixion and Resurrection of Christ... the cross, the ability of God to cope with this ultimate question of the mind and the heart, this ability to do this by suffering himself lifts it out of time and space into eternity. This doesn't mean to say that there are still not grave doubts and pains and despairs to be coped with' (Harries, 2001: 66).

These pains, doubts and despairs explode onto the page with the volume *H'm* (1972a). The intuitions we have already seen, namely that if this world is God's creation, then God must in some sense be responsible for the suffering, are explicitly stated: 'He struck it / Those great blows it resounds / With still ... Nature bandaged / Its wounds' (1972a, 'Echoes': 4). But perhaps the God is not, after all, the one who wounds, but the one who is wounded? Cain challenges God as to why Abel's offering was preferable to his own:

> And God said: It was part of myself
> He gave me. The lamb was torn
> From my own side. The limp head,
> The slow fall of red tears – they

Were like a mirror to me in which I beheld
My reflection. I anointed myself
In readiness for the journey
To the doomed tree you were at work upon. (1972a, 'Cain': 15)

D. Z. Phillips comments on this poem as follows:

Slowly, but surely, R. S. Thomas asks us to reflect on a God very different from the omnipotent sovereign bestowed with power to do what he chooses. At the door of such a god we bring our myriad questions concerning what went wrong with his plans. And to silence us we are told that the plan is more complex than we thought. It is in this context that 'the grovelling of theologians' flourish, and, let it be said, there are plenty of contemporary philosophers of religion to keep them company. But the God the poet would have us see in the poems we are considering now, seems to be one whose nature is involved with these very features of human life which we want explained away. This is a God who can be crucified. (1986: 80)

This is far from those atonement theories in which we see God in control, producing a solution. This is a vulnerable God, a God also vulnerable to rejected love:

I slept and dreamed
Of a likeness, fashioning it,
When I woke, to a slow
Music; in love with it
For itself, giving it freedom
To love me; risking the disappointment. (1972a, 'Making': 17)

There is a simplicity in some of R. S. Thomas's poetry that masks the depth of his theological understanding of the dilemmas with which he is wrestling and with which we wrestle. The God of whom R. S. Thomas speaks in 'Echoes', a violent wounding God, is set in counterpoint with a God who loves in generosity, loves the world for 'itself' and not for anything it can do or achieve, but will let that world go in freedom so that if it loves, it is not as a result of compulsion. God takes the risk that it will all end in disappointment, envisages that it could all end in the fall of 'red tears' as the dying lamb lies with lolling head.

The world is a small and vulnerable place: 'And God held in his hand / A small globe. Look, he said. / The son looked.' The scene is not promising:

> On a bare
> Hill a bare tree saddened
> The sky. Many people
> Held out their thin arms
> To it, as though waiting
> For a vanished April
> To return to its crossed
> Boughs. The son watched
> Them. Let me go there, he said. (1972a, 'The Coming': 35)

We remember from R. S. Thomas's earlier poetry that April speaks of resurrection, but this April seems to be dim memory, for the tree is bare and shows no signs of rebirth. There is an inchoate longing. The son watches. Is the son, having looked at the globe held in God's hand, going to turn his back on the wretched scene? No, there is a willingness to go, almost a pleading to be allowed to be part of the scene. 'Let me go there, he said' are such simple words, such profound and tender sentiments.

But there is a turbulent, destructive force also present in the poetry of this volume. Instead of the world being set free to love in freedom, 'Other' tells of the one termed 'He', who admires the work of his creation but then gets jealous of its independence. Onto the scene comes the machine 'singing to itself / Of money'. The machine becomes for R. S. Thomas more than an emblem of technology but is symbolic of a destructive force that ensnares people. It has a life of its own that seems indestructible. And God seems to be as helpless as humankind before the monster:

> God secreted
> A tear. Enough, enough,
> He commanded, but the machine
> Looked at him and went on singing. (1972a, 'Other': 36)

This is a confusing God, or perhaps it is us that are confused, imagining God in so many different ways. Thomas tells of a God who turns his back on humankind, repelled by its grin, and says

I'll mark you, he thought. He put his finger
On him. The result was poetry:
The lament of Job, Aeschylus,
The grovelling of the theologians.
Man went limping through life, holding
His side... .

It was not his first time to be crucified. (1972a, 'Repeat': 26)

As we noticed earlier, the pain produces the poetry. Job laments, Jacob
fights, humanity is wounded – and yet it appears that in the wounded
ones, is also the crucified one. R. S. Thomas appears to be experimenting
with language, imagery and the alternative views of God. Which one is
right? There seems to be no answer for him at this stage. All he knows
is that we are bent on creating destructive forces and 'Over the creeds /
And masterpieces our wheels go' (1972a, 'No Answer': 7).

Yet amongst these intellectual torments, the natural world has still the
power to refresh him. Walking by the river he hears the fish 'speckled
like thrushes, / Silently singing':

I bring the heart
Not the mind to the interpretation
Of their music, letting the stream
Comb me, feeling it fresh
In my veins, revisiting the sources
That are as near now
As on the morning I set out from them. (1972a, 'The River': 23)

We have in the volume *H'm* Thomas questioning at the level of the
mind, but the mind produces 'No Answer', the title of a poem in which
he says, 'But the chemicals in / My mind were not / Ready' (1972a: 7).
The heart, however, seems to be in advance of the mind, and knows
a cleansing, a nearness to a morning source (with its echoes of the
resurrection morning) that his intellect cannot appropriate.

There is another world, which is a long way off, where the industrial
machinery has been converted, for

industry is for mending
The bent bones and the minds fractured
By life. It's a long way off, but to get
There takes no time and admission
Is free, if you will purge yourself
Of desire, and present yourself with
Your need only and the simple offering
Of your faith, green as a leaf. (1972a, 'The Kingdom': 34)

The poetry of *H'm* is profoundly challenging to a comfortable Christianity. Even for R. S. Thomas, the expressions of alternative viewpoints are put in extreme form. But the power of poetry is that it does not ask for a purely intellectual engagement with dilemmas; it takes the reader into the world of these proposals, so they can be explored intuitively, with the heart as well as the reason.

After the storm tossed seas of *H'm* we reach the slightly calmer waters of the *Laboratories of the Spirit* (1975) – but not much calmer, for the questions are as penetrating as ever and we come to the poem 'Amen' (1975: 5), about which Dyson speculated, 'I am tempted to wonder what poet or sceptic could write a more effective anti-Christian poem, if he wanted to' (1990: 274). It is in 'Amen' that R. S. Thomas has engaged most directly with atonement theory, as popularly understood. Can we *really* say 'Amen' to the views expressed in this poem, or is it heavily ironic?

It was all arranged:
the virgin with child, the birth
in Bethlehem, the arid journey uphill
to Jerusalem. The prophets foretold
it, the scriptures conditioned him
to accept it. Judas went to his work
with his sour kiss; what else
could he do?
    A wise old age,
the honours awarded for lasting,
are not for a saviour. He had
to be killed; salvation acquired
by an increased guilt. The tree,
with its roots in the mind's dark,
was divinely planted, the original fork

in existence. There is no meaning in life,
unless men can be found to reject
love. God needs his martyrdom.
The mild eyes stare from the Cross
in perverse triumph. What does he care
that the people's offerings are so small?

'A flawed creation; a flawed salvation?' poses Dyson (1990: 273).
It is difficult to be sure exactly what R. S. Thomas is saying in this
poem: the reader's own presuppositions will undoubtedly influence the
interpretation. But it seems as though Thomas has taken atonement
theory that requires a death, which has it all set down as a pre-arranged
plan, and says: 'This is what such a theory looks like in practice. Do
you agree with that?' Phillips' comment seems relevant here: 'In face
of the varied aspects of human life, there has always been a deep desire
among certain religious believers to discover a pattern which will make
sense of the whole. One of the ways in which this has been done is
to assume or postulate a divine plan in which everything has its place.
R. S. Thomas is too honest and too perceptive a poet to be able to give
assent to such a notion of complete and final explanations' (1986: 42).
Whatever the meaning of the cross, the final explanation of 'Amen'
seems unacceptable.

And what a haunting sense of isolation is created by the poem 'The
Word' (1975: 3). Words are about communication, bridging gaps,
bringing people together, but not in this poem:

A pen appeared, and the god said:
'Write what it is to be
man.' And my hand hovered
long over the bare page,

until there, like footprints
of the lost traveller, letters
took shape on the page's
blankness, and I spelled out

the word 'lonely'. And my hand moved
to erase it; but the voices
of all those waiting at life's
window cried out loud: 'It is true.'

When R. S. Thomas reads that poem himself on the recording by Sain (1999), the last three words, 'It is true' echo the hooting call of an owl giving it an eerie quality. But perhaps, despite his reluctance to write the word 'lonely', or allow it to remain on the page, the poet feels that he has a duty to all those who are on the margins to acknowledge the truth of how lonely it can be to be human. With an ironic twist, the word that is communicated is that we are lonely yet we stand with and for others who experience this loneliness, those who are 'waiting'.

Yet there can be shared moments that are timeless, outstrip our words, that put the banality of our lives into perspective:

> I served on a dozen committees;
> talked hard, said little ...
> >   One particular
> time after a harsh morning
> of rain, the clouds lifted, the wind
> fell; there was a resurrection
> of nature, and we there to emerge
> with it into the anointed
> air. I wanted to say to you: 'We
> will remember this.' But tenses
> were out of place on that green
> island, ringed with the rain's
> bow, that we had found and would spend
> the rest of our lives looking for. (1975: 'That Place': 8)

The dynamic is still present, swinging from darkness, failure to answer the questions of life, isolation and loneliness, to a 'resurrection' experience, one that was shared with another, and all things are put in perspective. There is that sense of being able to step into 'the kingdom' through the thinnest of veils, and know that one is in another place, which is still nevertheless in this world.

There can come an illumination which the heart can experience, which comes as gift, although paradoxically, the seeking, thinking, exploring are still necessary. As with the psalmist who moves from lament to praise, without there being an apparent logical explanation for that movement, so too resurrection comes and the world, which remains the same, is transformed. The poet experiences blessing in the whole of his being, overflowing with the presence of Christ as though he were the chalice, that vessel used for the blood of Christ, into which the sea is being poured (1975, 'Suddenly': 32).

As we have examined the poetry of R. S. Thomas, we have not spent time on the mechanics of how the line breaks add to the overall effect, but they are a significant factor in the experience of reading the poem. In this next poem I have added suggestions in brackets of the thoughts that the line breaks, by coming where they do, might provoke. Helen Vendler has pointed out (in M. W. Thomas, 1993: 65) that undertaking such an exercise shows how the line-breaks 'tend to make us replicate the process of interpretation, with its constant hesitation and rephrasings':

As I had always known (Known? Can we know? Is this going to
be bad?)
he would come, unannounced, (If his coming is unannounced,
how can we know he is coming)
remarkable merely for the absence (Ah, he is to be absent again?)
of clamour. So the truth must appear (Oh, it is the absence of
clamour.)
to the thinker; so at a stage (The truth just appears, as gift, but it is
to the thinker?)
of the experiment, the answer (So we are going to get an answer to
our thought experiments?)
must quietly emerge. I looked (Looking, not thinking?)
at him, not with the eye (Why not the eye?)
only, but with the whole (Ah, not the eye only, but the whole, but
whole what?)
of my being, overflowing with (Overflowing with what?)
him as a chalice would (With him! As a chalice, the vessel of
sorrow and joy?)
with the sea ... (With the sea!! This is a very different sort of
'answer'.)
(1975, 'Suddenly': 32)

What hyperbole, overflowing as a chalice would with the sea! The words echo the 23rd Psalm, 'my cup runneth over', but now the cup is his body and the running over is not just a trickle, but a deluge. R. S. Thomas often appears spare, restrained, pared to the bone, but there can also be an affluence, a bodily delight and resurrection in his poetry. This is one such occasion.

The light, so important for R. S. Thomas, is still radiant on fleeting occasions, but the occasion has to be seized, not ignored, and be treasured:

I have seen the sun break through
to illuminate a small field
for a while, and gone my way
and forgotten it. But that was the pearl
of great price, the one field that had
the treasure in it. I realize now
that I must give all that I have
to possess it. (1975, 'The Bright Field', 60)

Or it can be found in a little used country church. 'I keep my eyes /
open and am not dazzled, / so delicately does the light enter / my soul'
(1975, 'Llananno': 62).

As we have come to expect, however, such exaltation, such setting
aside of the questions, such resurrection extravagance, does not appear
to last in this world. The old problems re-emerge when he confronts life
as it is actually lived:

And in the book I read:
God is love. But lifting
my head, I do not find it
so. (1975, 'Which': 54)

Yet despite all this see-sawing from one extreme to another, the
beginning and end of this further book of experimentation, for the
collection is called *Laboratories of the Spirit*, have intimations of hope.
The first poem in the book is 'Emerging' (1975: 1) and what emerges is
that prayer is not about pounding God with a 'shrill cry', but learning
that prayer is about 'the annihilation of difference, / the consciousness of
myself in you, / of you in me'. We have to learn to grow up, to be tested
in the 'laboratory of the spirit', perhaps in the way Job (and even Christ?)
experienced testing.

The final word in the book, in the poem 'Good', reverts back to
consideration of the hill farmer. The old man knows his life is nearing
the end. But

His grandson is there
ploughing; his young wife fetches him
cakes and tea and a dark smile. It is well. (1975: 65)

Here, in a simple poem, R. S. Thomas is still able to combine the chill of death as the man anticipates his own demise and sees the kestrel 'with fresh prey / in its claws', with the sense that in the rhythm of life there may not be answers but there is the overarching sense that 'It is well', with its echoes of that reassurance Julian of Norwich famously received.

And there are just some occasions when a great paean of praise comes from his lips, as in the aptly titled 'Praise' in the volume *The Way of It*:

I praise you because
you are artist and scientist
in one... .
You run off your scales of
rain water and sea water, play
the chords of the morning
and evening light, sculpture
with shadow, join together leaf
by leaf, when spring
comes, the stanzas of
an immense poem. You speak
all languages and none,
answering our most complex
prayers with the simplicity
of a flower, ...   (1977, 'Praise': 20)

On occasions, R. S. Thomas would write poetry relating to his wife and their marriage. There are indications that at times things could be a little strained between them, although his poems of love in old age are touchingly beautiful and tender. In the title poem 'The Way Of It' there is a recognition that the tears of life extend to their relationship for 'She is at work / always, mending the garment / of our marriage'. But whether the commencement of their marriage was in some way inauspicious, and whether there can sometimes be sharp words, nevertheless his wife sacrifices herself by bearing his burdens for 'If there are thorns / in my life, it is she who / will press her breast to them and sing' (1977: 30). The reference echoes the tale of how the robin got his red breast by being pierced by the thorns ringing Christ's head. Love, loss, redemption are part of the intimate relationships of life.

Frequencies, the last volume to be published in the 1970s, continues R. S. Thomas's quest for answers, straining eyes and ears to apprehend vibrations of the divine. The opening poem is not encouraging to the quest – 'The Gap' (1978: 7,8) seems to be a distance maintained deliberately by God. But Thomas goes on 'Fishing':

The water is deep. Sometimes from far
down invisible messages arrive.
Often it seems it is for more than fish
that we seek; we wait for the

withheld answer to an insoluble
problem.

Undeterred 'we fish on' and there is a catch of a sort for the bodies accumulate 'in the torn / light that is about us and the air / echoes to their inaudible screaming' (1978: 'Fishing'; 11). If the fish we catch are meant to be answers, then these are disturbing answers for it consists of bodies screaming at a level our ears do not pick up – and the light is torn.

Turning over the page to 'Groping' (1978: 12) the sense of feeling one's way in the dark, continues: 'For some / it is all darkness; for me, too, / it is dark'. But there is a glimmer of hope, for he finds that 'there are hands / there I can take, voices to hear' and a gleam of a strange light 'that is / the halo upon the bones / of the pioneers who died for truth.' Those voices of counter-testimony, who suffered in their quest, are here recognized as even yet providing a hope for future generations. We have to listen hard for those voices, strain our eyes to catch the light that has been shed and continues to be shed by those pioneers who have gone ahead in the search for truth, and died, literally or metaphorically, for that truth. Those pioneers include the psalmist, the writer of Job and, supremely, the Jesus of history. But we have to take their hands if we are also to be helped.

The search for truth requires bravery, however. R. S. Thomas considers whether, afraid to go out into the open, we shelter behind our theoretical constructions, our formalized belief systems: 'I will open / my eyes on a world where the problems / remain but our doctrines / protect us' (1978, 'Shadows': 25). For himself, he has decided not to take such shelter, to venture out on a perilous unprotected journey: 'I have abandoned / my theories, the easier certainties / of belief. There are no handrails to / grasp' (1978, 'Balance': 49).

The poem 'Balance' is inspired by the writings of Kierkegaard, who is specifically named in the poem. The balance of faith is a difficult one to maintain over 'seventy thousand fathoms'. The waters are deep. To be a person of faith requires (lonely) courage. Kierkegaard writes:

> In suffering and tribulation there are really certain situations in which, humanly speaking, the thought of God and that he is nevertheless love, makes the suffering far more exhausting. . . Humanly speaking one who suffered and was tried thus would be justified in saying: it would all be less painful to me if I did not at the same time have the idea of God. For either one suffers at the thought that God the all-powerful, who could so easily help, leaves one helpless, or else one suffers because one's reason is crucified by the thought that God is love all the same and that what happens to one is for one's good... Despair makes everything easier because it is an undisturbed agreement with oneself that the suffering is unbearable.' (quoted in Lethbridge and O'Grady, 2002: 116)

'Reason is crucified': this could be a title for Thomas's poem 'The Empty Church'. As the priest kneels yet again in an empty church, he imagines the candles as lures for some giant moth of a God:

Ah, he had burned himself
before in the human flame
and escaped, *leaving the reason
torn*. He will not come any more

to our lure. Why, then, do I kneel still
striking my prayers on a stone
heart? Is it in hope one
of them will ignite and throw
on its illumined walls the shadow
of someone greater than I can understand? (1978, 'The Empty Church: 35, my emphasis)

Why had God in Christ come, what was the reason, the meaning of his life and death? Our Reason, our mental faculties, are torn by the mystery. Is the reason we do not comprehend precisely because we imagine we can domesticate the God who is beyond human understanding? But there is still hope that we might just catch the shadow of such a God if we continue diligently to seek him, although we cannot expect a full illumination, or can we? Is there an answer, and what sort of answer is it?

And slowly the questions
occur, vague but formidable
for all that. We pass our hands
over their surface like blind
men, feeling for the mechanism
that will swing them aside. They
yield, but only to re-form
as new problems; and one
does not even do that
but towers immovable
before us.
        Is there no way
other than thought of answering
its challenge? There is an anticipation
of it to the point of
dying. There have been times
when, after long on my knees
in a cold chancel, a stone has rolled
from my mind, and I have looked
in and seen the old questions lie
folded and in a place
by themselves, like the piled
graveclothes of love's risen body. (1978, 'The Answer': 46)

What is this one question, which 'towers immovable' and will not
yield? McGill suggests it is the cross (2004: 199). If we are unable to
get round this one, insoluble, problem by thought, by theorizing, is there
another way? After a long time praying in church (and R. S. Thomas
describes the same experience mediated through nature, *Autobiographies*,
1997a: 84,122) the stone rolls from his *mind*, and he sees the graveclothes
of his questioning, folded, put to one side.

William Davis (in M. W. Thomas, 1993: 111) speculates whether
the line break at 'lie' is meant to suggest that the questions are false,
inappropriate, or intended to deceive. In any case, it seems that, in the
light of the resurrected Christ, the questions, for that moment, just do
not matter any more, are simply not relevant. Again, as we have noted
before, it is in looking, in a visionary experience, that the answer comes.
But we must be careful not to imagine that the 'answer' is the neatly

packaged type of answer we might crave. Is the title of the poem ironic, subverting our normal search for answers? If the 'old questions' are set to one side, is it new questions we need rather than no questions at all? The experience was not just an isolated one, for 'there have been times', but it is told retrospectively and implies that it is difficult to live continuously as 'resurrection people'.

There is a form of intelligence that does not come through reason. Mark Wynn has argued for the idea that 'emotional feelings can themselves carry intellectual content. I also argue that in some cases, this content may not be otherwise available, in which case feeling's role may not just be constructive, but indispensable' (2005: xi). R. S. Thomas has suggested, in his poem 'Perhaps', 'To learn to distrust the distrust / of feeling – this then was the next step / for the seeker?' (1978: 39).

In his search to find the frequency on which God operates there are many difficulties. R. S. Thomas has taken up the voice of counter-testimony in the search for truth; he will not be silent about the difficulties of belief, or the character of God. He imagines himself as a latter day Job in 'At It':

> And I would have
> things to say to this God
> at the judgement, storming at him,
> as Job stormed, with the eloquence
> of the abused heart. (1978: 15)

Yet he always goes on searching. In his disorientation he looks for new orientation. In the crucifying absence of God, he hungers for a resurrection of the spirit. Absence is not the same as non-existence, because absence speaks of a presence that is missing. 'An absence is how we become surer / of what we want', as Thomas says in his poem 'Abercuawg' (1978: 26). There is a passionate intensity for God underlying the spare words of some of Thomas's writings. And there is hope, too. In the poem 'The Absence' it would appear, to begin with, that there is no hope, that he will never catch up with his God, that he will always just miss him. But the poem ends with these words:

> What resource have I
> other than the emptiness without him of my whole
> being, a vacuum he may not abhor? (1978, 'The Absence': 48)

'Nature abhors a vacuum', so it seems natural to conclude that he will again experience that overflowing presence he spoke of earlier in 'Suddenly'. But also we recall those words we sing at Christmas in the carol 'O come, all ye faithful': 'God of God, Light of Light, lo, he abhors not the Virgin's womb'. Thomas brings only his emptiness, and with words which are not meant to be presumptuous, nevertheless suggests that a resurrection experience will be his, a rebirth of assurance in God.

Chapter Seven
Destinations

R. S. Thomas was totally serious about his calling as a poet. In his diary of *A Year in Llŷn* Thomas notes 'For me, being a poet is a full-time job, and although the muse may languish as one grows older, there is a kind of duty upon you to persevere in perfecting your craft, and to secure an answer, through poetry, to some of the great questions of life' (*Autobiographies*, 1997a: 150). He had an objective, he was on a journey, and there are destinations in view. But the directions for that journey are hard to read:

> In this desert of language
> > we find ourselves in,
> with the sign-post with the word 'God'
> > worn away
> > > > and the distance ...? (1981, 'Directions': 81)

And although he might have a willingness to follow the directions, if he could read them, nevertheless the signpost resonates with the arms of the cross, so that it casts a shadow over any optimistic embracing of the future:

> > I am one of those
> who sees from the arms opened
> > > to embrace the future
> the shadow of the Cross fall
> > on the smoothest of surfaces
> > > > causing me to stumble. (1981, 'Directions': 81)

The shadow of the cross roughs up life's surface. It is a problem that will not go away. There is a price to pay, suggests Thomas, a penance for the creation of humanity, for humanity continuously falls short of what it could be: 'I feel sometimes / we are his penance / for having made us' (1981, 'Covenant': 82). Humanity sins, and God pays the price. This is not to endorse the technicalities of the penal substitution theory of atonement, but it affirms that somehow God suffers for our sins. But if humanity and God are inextricably linked in a covenant relationship, then the suffering of the one is the suffering of the other, so this also means that the mutual indwelling leads to the participation of humanity in the suffering of God: 'He / suffers in us and we partake / of his suffering' (1981, 'Covenant': 82). William McGill says of 'Covenant', 'The poem bristles with the sense of man's affinity for sin, and, like so many of Thomas's poems, has at least the shadow of the shadow of the Cross cast across its lines. Implicit is the Atonement. It is not an easy doctrine, but one that Thomas came at time and again, sometimes directly, sometimes obliquely, never quite embracing joyously, but never able to turn away from it' (2004: 109).

This is the paradox: that atonement is about making us at one with God, which is our greatest joy, but it is also a unity with the one who suffers. This knowledge continuously informs R. S. Thomas's poetry of crucifixion and resurrection. But we need to redefine 'knowledge' when it comes to understanding God. D. Z. Phillips says:

> Men who believe in a self-emptying God can only worship him by sharing his nature... As long as we think of God as providing explanatory answers for the world's ills, this religious insight will elude us. We think of knowledge as power and control. God's knowledge is then thought of as supreme power and control. The kind of knowledge of God R. S. Thomas wants to show us in his poetry is very different. This knowledge is only possible through a sacrifice, a dying to the self, so that God can come in at the right place. The seeker of justifications of the ways of God to men wants to know why things happened to him in just the ways they did. The man who comes to see that no such reasons can be found, who sees the givenness of his life as an act of grace, has come to a knowledge of God. (1986: 83)

So what can one do, what progress can one make along life's road, in the face of the challenges of life and faith? 'Waiting' is the suggestion, the title of the next poem in the collection: waiting for God to answer when God wills and not when we demand it:

      Now
in the small hours
of belief the one eloquence

to master is that

of the bowed head, the bent
knee, waiting, as at the end

of a hard winter
for one flower to open
on the mind's tree of thorns. (1981, 'Waiting': 83)

As we wait through the winter night, where silence in prayer before
God is eloquence, we have the promise that there will be an 'end' to this,
a destination, and that it will be in the springtime of an opening flower.
But the flower opens on a tree of thorns with its crucifixion imagery.
The new orientation of resurrection will be a flowering of the suffering
(and in this case the suffering is the mental one of difficult questioning)
but the implication is that the flower cannot be plucked from the tree of
thorns without withering.

In 'Voices' R. S. Thomas tells of the two voices which cause such
tension in him:

Who to believe?
The linnet sings bell-like,
a tinkling music. It says life
is contained here; is a jewel

in a shell casket, lying
among down. There is another
voice, far out in space,
whose persuasiveness is the distance

from which it speaks. Divided
mind, the message is always
in two parts. Must it be
on a cross it is made one? (1981, 'Voices': 91)

The linnet's voice is 'bell-like' giving the impression that it is true
and it is a precious treasure. Yet there are some references that indicate
that all is perhaps not so positive, for a tinkling music is fragile and
ephemeral, a casket can have resonances of death, and the emphasis
given to 'lying' through its position at the end of the line, makes for
hesitation over the truthfulness of that voice. And what of the voice far

out in space? Is this the voice that overwhelms with the immensity of the heavens – but it is distant, and perhaps indistinct? Do we have here two voices, one speaking from things of the earth, one from things of the heavens, and this creates tension in the mind, creates a divided mind? 'Who to believe?'

Are things of earth and heaven brought together in unity in the cross, and *must* it be that way? The cross draws Thomas back again and again with the intuition that here is a pivotal point for understanding those tensions that split the mind. 'Divided mind, the message is always in two parts' could be an apt summary of Thomas's poetry. At an intellectual level he never resolves those tensions, yet at the level of faith the cross seems to bring a resolution that defies analysis.

The theme of voices continues in the poem 'Threshold'. The Old Testament prophet Elijah (1 Kings 19) emerged from *his* dark cave, and found that the Lord was not in the wind, earthquake or fire that passed by, but he did eventually hear God's word of direction and encouragement in the still small voice. For R. S. Thomas, Elijah's experiences are repeated but, unlike Elijah, the still small voice does not bring encouragement:

I emerge from the mind's
cave into the worse darkness
outside, where things pass and
the Lord is in none of them.

I have heard the still, small voice
and it was that of the bacteria
demolishing my cosmos. I
have lingered too long on

this threshold, but where can I go? (1981, 'Threshold': 110)

As Thomas seeks for the destination to which he should be travelling he is paralyzed by inactivity, hesitating on the threshold, realizing he should be moving on, but unsure of the way. In the absence of clear direction, of known paths, he can only hope and trust. 'What // to do but, like Michelangelo's /Adam, put my hand / out into unknown space, / hoping for the reciprocating touch?' (1981, 'Threshold': 110). The interior life of the mind is dark, the observed world is darker still, the experience of the faithful of old as told in the Bible is subverted, but still Thomas reaches out, hoping against hope that he will be helped forward on his journey.

But there are times on this difficult journey when the disorientation he often experiences is swept away in a spirit of newness – the old world of disharmony is replaced by harmonic praise. And it comes 'Suddenly', the second poem with this same title, which speaks of God's in-breaking. He now hears clearly a voice pouring forth, not in a dribble but a gush. And what is strange is that those very things that had before seemed to speak against belief and hope, now are united in praise of God:

Suddenly after long silence
he has become voluble.
He addresses me from a myriad
directions with the fluency
of water, the articulateness
of green leaves; and in the genes,
too, the components
of my existence. The rock,
so long speechless, is the library
of his poetry....
     I have no need
to despair; as at
some second Pentecost
of a Gentile, I listen to the things
around me: weeds, stones, instruments,
the machine itself, all
speaking to me in the vernacular
of the purposes of One who is. (1983a, 'Suddenly': 201)

Can all things be redeemed? It would seem that all things, baptized in the Spirit, can speak to the poet in a language he can understand 'of the purposes of the One who is'. Pentecost (Acts 2) is the time when the reality of the risen Jesus came home to the gathered crowds; it was the time of empowerment, when despair and disillusion was transformed into joy. It was the time for repentance, turning around to face in a different direction; a time when the message began its explosive journey out from Jerusalem to the Gentile world. This new orientation recognizes that there has been despair in the past, that there have been crucifixion experiences. Now however is the time of resurrection, new beginnings. The world has not changed, the 'machine' is still there after all, but the transformation has occurred in the poet.

Arrival, reaching a destination, is possible, it seems:

Not conscious
    that you have been seeking
      suddenly
    you come upon it

the village in the Welsh hills
    dust free
with no road out
but the one you came in by.

    A bird chimes
    from a green tree
the hour that is no hour
    you know. The river dawdles
to hold a mirror for you
where you may see yourself
    as you are, a traveller
      with the moon's halo
    above him, who has arrived
    after long journeying where he
      began, catching this
    one truth by surprise
that there is everything to look forward to. (1983a, 'Arrival': 203)

The traveller can see himself in the reflection in the slow moving river as someone, not no-one, for the reality is that the celestial bodies have granted the human to be haloed. The arrival is not consciously planned, the destination has not been deliberately sought, but is gift, grace. The long journey has been circular, for he is back where he started. But he is surprised by the knowledge, the truth, 'that there is everything to look forward to'.

The need some have to leave the familiar in order to explore the reality of faith in new ways is witnessed to by Mike Riddell, Mark Pierson and Cathy Kirkpatrick in their book *The Prodigal Project, Journey into the emerging church,* but they conclude that the way may indeed lead back to the beginning. Does this negate the need to journey? This is not how they see it, because the journey is where change takes place:

Perhaps it is a circular trip, like that of the Prodigal the project is named after, and we will arrive eventually not far from where we started. But if that is the case, we will be very different people. And the voyage will have been essential. This one fact we know: our journey is toward Love. What we have left behind is insignificant compared to that which we are approaching. (2000: 140,141)

Destinations is the title of a slim volume by Thomas, published in a limited edition as a collector's item by The Celandine Press in 1985. It commences with 'The Message':

A message from God
delivered by a bird
at my window, offering friendship.
Listen. Such language!
Who said God was without
speech? Every word an injection
to make me smile. (1985: 7)

'Who said God was without speech?' – well Thomas for one! 'Who ever heard Him speak? We have to live virtually the whole of our lives in the presence of an invisible and mute God' Thomas says in *Neb*, his autobiography. However he goes on to say 'But that was never a bar to anyone seeking to come into contact with Him. That is what prayer is' (1997a: 104). And his prayer is answered, for he hears God in the voice of the bird. 'Offering friendship'! This is a surprise from R. S. Thomas, for he had said, in his introduction to his selection, *A Choice of George Herbert's Verse*, that Herbert demonstrates 'the possibility and the desirability of a friendship with God. Friendship is no longer the right way to describe it. The word now is dialogue, encounter, confrontation; but the realities engaged have not altered all that much' (1967: 16). But now Thomas is speaking of the possibility of friendship with God.

The song/words are, however, an injection, an anaesthetic. In the real world, one lives without the benefit of anaesthetic, can such messages of hope and friendship still be received? It seems they might, for the poem ends with the words 'Meet me, tomorrow, / I say, and I will sing it all over / again for you, when you have come to.'

The title poem 'Destinations' suggests that we do have a goal in view, although it is easy to get waylaid: 'Travelling towards the light / we were waylaid by darkness'. The poem concludes by further defining the light-filled destination:

> to the light, yes,

> but not such as minerals
> deploy; to the brightness over
> an interior horizon, which is science
> transfiguring itself in love's mirror. (1985: 18)

Science, at least science as it is applied in technical innovation, Thomas generally sees as being in opposition to the things that make for life. Here though science is pictured as being transfigured by love and providing an illuminating aura.

Is the journey then a linear one, or a circular one? 'Cones', in the collection *Experimenting with an Amen* (1986) provides a more nuanced reply: it is a spiral:

> Heartening that in our journeys
> through time we come round not
> to the same place, but recognise it
> from a distance. It is the dream
> we remember, that makes us say:
> 'We have been here before.' In
> truth we are as far from it
> as one side of the cone
> from the other, and in between
> are the false starts, the failures,
> the ruins from which we climbed,
> not to look down, but to feel your glance
> resting on us at the next angle
> of the gyre.
>   God, it is not your reflections
> we seek, wonderful as they are
> in the live fibre; it is the possibility
> of your presence at the cone's
> point towards which we soar
> in hope to arrive at the still
> centre, where love operates

on all those frequencies
that are set up by the spinning
of two minds, the one on the other. (1986: 3)

We have been looking for a dynamic in the poetry of R. S. Thomas taking him through from disorientation to a new orientation, echoing the experience and language of crucifixion and resurrection. Yet we have also found on the journeying that there can be a sense of return. 'Cones' gives an insight into how we might envisage this movement. The sense of spiraling up resonates with Karen Armstrong's description of her spiritual journey in her autobiographical book *The Spiral Staircase*, which she elucidates with reference to Eliot. Hers is eventually a journey through to resurrection, although for a considerable stretch of time that outcome seemed in doubt:

> In Eliot's *Ash-Wednesday*, we watch the poet painfully climbing a spiral staircase. This image is reflected in the twisting sentences of the verse, which often revolves upon itself, repeating the same words and phrases, apparently making little headway, but pushing steadily forwards nevertheless. My own life has progressed in the same way. For years it seemed a hard Lenten journey, but without the prospect of Easter. I toiled round and round in pointless circles, covering the same ground, repeating the same mistakes, quite unable to see where I was going. Yet all the time, without realizing it, I was slowly climbing out of the darkness... For a long time, I assumed that I had finished with religion for ever, yet, in the end, the strange and seemingly arbitrary revolutions of my life led me to the kind of transformation that, I now believe, was what I had been seeking all those years ago when I packed my suitcase, entered my convent and set off to find God. (2005: 15)

'Cones' seems to be a profoundly hopeful poem. It recognizes the 'false starts, the failures' but these are left behind as the ascent is continued, not as a lonely figure but in company, for it is 'we' who are travelling. God's glance (not a steady gaze admittedly) rests on us as we turn the next corner and the implication is that this is a benign regard. Unusually for R. S. Thomas, the poem is also addressed to God rather than about God. The prayer is an audacious one, too: not simply to see God's reflection in the created world, wonderful as that is, but it is in the hope of being lifted up, soaring, into the presence of God at the 'cone's point'. The divided mind, the message in two parts, the contraries of heart and head, find a unity in this destination of love. This is resurrection.

But of course R. S. Thomas does not rest here. Later in the same collection is the complex poem 'Revision' (1986: 22,23). 'So the catechism begins' with two voices, one interrogating the other. Is the second voice doing revision, swotting, or is it altering, revising, the standard orthodoxies of belief, for at one point the first voice accuses the other of blasphemy? But the poem is worth wrestling with because it gives insights into R. S. Thomas's core experience of faith. Rowan Williams says of the poem:

> It is never easy to tease out what Thomas might understand by 'salvation'. Most of the conventional Christian thoughts about this are at best unspoken in his work. But if one turns to the gnomically intense 'Revision', one finds a kind of definition, if not exactly of 'salvation', then of that life or awareness that faith creates. (In D. W. Davies, 2003: 214)

Taking up the poem at the mid-point, with the first voice, the questioner, speaking:

>   'Life's simpleton,
> know this gulf you have created
> can be crossed by prayer. Let me hear
> if you can walk it.'
>   'I have walked it.
> It is called silence, and is a rope
>   over an unfathomable
> abyss, which goes on and on
> never arriving.'
>   'So that your Amen
> is unsaid. Know, friend, the arrival
> is the grace given to maintain
> your balance, the power which supplies
> not the maggot of flame you desired,
> that consumes the flesh, but the unseen
> current between two points, coming
> to song in the nerves, as in the telegraph
> wires, the tighter that they are drawn.'

We may prefer a life of faith, of salvation, to exist in an absence of tension, to be in union with God with no struggle. We may prefer our destination to be clear and achievable, not to be endlessly journeying, never arriving. This poem suggests that grace is being able to keep your balance whilst walking the tightrope over the abyss, that this is not in fact failure but a form of arrival. Tension suggests that the wire is firmly anchored at two points, that the other, though far off, is not absent, and that the greater the tension, the more productive it is. The word used is 'song', suggesting perhaps that this is the gifted music of the one particularly in tune with the divine Other.

Perhaps the reference here is to those who have been especially called to wrestle with the intractable dilemmas of religious life and bring that to the world: the prophets and poets, the voices of counter-testimony. This coheres with a comment Thomas makes in his autobiography *Neb* of his early experiences as a priest. 'At the time he was too young and too inexperienced to know that tension is an irremovable part of art' (1997a: 52). The poet/prophet may be called to know the sorrow of the world at a greater depth, be crucified, so that their gift, their song, may save others.

But a flock of birds open the door to a different way of seeing. In 'A Thicket in Lleyn' (1986: 45) the migratory birds mistake Thomas for a tree, he is so still:

> They would have perched
> on me, had I had nourishment
> in my fissures. As it was,
> they netted me in their shadows,
> brushed me with sound, feathering the arrows
> of their own bows, and were gone,
> leaving me to reflect on the answer
> to a question I had not asked.
> 'A repetition in time of the eternal
> I AM.' Say it. Don't be shy.
> Escape from your mortal cage
> in thought. Your migrations will never
> be over. Between two truths
> there is only the mind to fly with.
> Navigate by such stars as are not
> leaves falling from life's

deciduous tree, but spray from the fountain
of the imagination, endlessly
replenishing itself out of its own waters.

It is Coleridge and his understanding of the Imagination that is the
reference here. The birds, appealing to Thomas's imagination rather than
his rational analysis, unwittingly provide an answer. There is always
going to be a movement from one point to the other, the migrations, the
journeying will go on, but the guiding star for the journey is to be found
not in decay but in the fountain of the imagination, which will not run
dry. The poet tells of the crucifying experiences but also of the times of
resurrection.

In 'This One' (1986: 58) he reflects further on his journeying:

Sometimes a shadow passed
between him and the light.
Sometimes a light showed itself
in the darkness beyond. Could
it be? The strong angels wrestled
and were not disposed to give
him the verdict. Are there journeys
without destinations? The animals
paused and became gargoyles
beside the way. And this one,
standing apart to confer
with the eternal, was he blamed
for reaction? There is always
laughter out of the speeding
vehicles for the man
who is still, half-way though he be
in a better direction. From receding
horizons he has withdrawn
his mind for greater repose
on an inner perspective,
where love is the bridge between
thought and time. (1986: 58)

R. S. Thomas is often thought of as a poet who is a stranger to love.
He does not deploy that word with easy familiarity, but it is still there in
his poetry and because the word does not come easily to his lips, when

it does occur it is more noticeable. 'Love is the bridge between thought and time'.

And love crops up in his unusual autobiographical collection of prose and poetry *The Echoes Return Slow* (1988). On one side is a prose reflection, matched on the opposite page by poetic interpretation, although the poetry can be rather tangential to the prose. His inadequacies as a pastor he confesses in prose:

> In an age of science everything is analysable but a tear. Everywhere he went, despite his round collar and his licence, he was there to learn rather than teach love. In the simplest of homes there were those who with little schooling and less college had come out top in that sweet examination. (1988: 92)

But, as we have already noted, the Eucharist was for him a precious moment. Was that a moment of love for him? 'The simplicity of the Sacrament absolved him from the complexities of the Word' (1988: 68), is his prose comment. The matching poem on the facing page suggests he brings a questioning love as he raises the chalice. He likens the chalice to a crystal, an object that not only reflects light, but perhaps suggests something in which one may see visions. However, he is drenched in light, so that he can no longer see. Is this an echo for Thomas of the Damascus Road experience of St Paul when he met the risen Christ and was blinded by the light (Acts 9:1-10)?

> The breaking of the wave
> outside echoed the breaking
> of bread in his hands.
>
> The crying of sea-gulls
> was the cry from the Cross:
> Lama Sabachthani. He lifted
>
> the chalice, that crystal in
> which love questioning is love
> blinded with excess of light. (1988: 69)

R. S. Thomas was more at home in the small churches of his rural ministry than the cathedrals, which he associated with a certain militarism, anathema to him as a pacifist: 'Is God worshipped only in cathedrals, where blood drips from regimental standards as from the crucified body of love' (1988: 82). The matching poem says:

> The church is small.
> The walls inside
> white. On the altar
> a cross, with behind it
> its shadow and behind
> that the shadow of its shadow.
>
> The world outside
> knows nothing of this
> nor cares. The two shadows
> are because of the shining
> of two candles: as many
> the lights, so many
> the shadows. So we learn
> something of the nature
> of God, the endlessness
> of whose recessions
> are brought up short by
> the contemporaneity of the Cross. (1988: 83)

The cross for R. S. Thomas is central, still relevant. That we do not find conventional theories of atonement in his writings does not mean that he is not struggling to find meaning in the cross. Along with him, as we read the poetry, we too struggle to find the meaning for the cross today. The answer, it would seem, is not in grasping its meaning with the intellect, but with the heart. His prayer to God, or rather the 'Anonymous presence', is to recognize that words alone, scientific exploration, will not be the means of answering his questions: 'Anonymous presence / grant that, when I come / questioning, it is not with the dictionary / in one hand, the microscope in the other' (1988: 115).

The final poem in the book is for his wife, Elsi, who in her last years suffered continuous ill health:

> I look out over the timeless sea
> over the head of one, calendar
> to time's passing, who is now open
> at the last month, her hair wintry.

Am I catalyst of her mettle that,
at my approach, her grimace of pain
turns to a smile? What it is saying is:
'Over love's depths only the surface is wrinkled.' (1988: 121)

The poem is about human relationships but it could also, it seems to me, apply to Thomas's relationship with his God. He speaks often of the abyss, the watery depths over which he has to balance in his walk with God. The surface of life is often torn, roughened, choppy as he views it in all its reality. By now R. S. Thomas was retired, still living on the Llŷn Peninsula, but in an ancient cottage at Sarn Rhiw overlooking a bay the English translation of which is Hell's Mouth. The retirement from active ministry did not mean retirement from questioning and searching, however; indeed it gave greater opportunities for the doubts to plague him. 'The problems he had concealed from his congregations had him now all to themselves' (1988: 112). As he journeys on, seeks the direction for this life and beyond this life, there seems to be an assurance here that the questionings belong to the surface, that pain turns to a smile in the presence of relationship, and that his wife's smile is telling him that 'over love's depths only the surface is wrinkled': this applies not only to their love, but in his relationship with his God.

Chapter Eight
No final arrival

In Karen Armstrong's book *The Case for God* (2009) she argues that in our modern world we have fallen prey to the idea that talking about God is easy, requires little effort. But this, she says, is a new idea for it used to be recognized by many in the pre-modern world that the contrary was the case; it is very difficult indeed to talk about God. Allied to this is the belief that religion is about providing answers:

> We have got used to thinking that religion should provide us with information. Is there a God? How did the world come into being? But this is a modern aberration. Religion was never supposed to provide answers to questions that lay within the reach of human reason. That was the role of *logos*. Religion's task, closely allied to that of art, was to help us to live creatively, peacefully and even joyously with realities for which there were no easy explanations and problems that we could not solve: mortality, pain, grief, despair, and outrage at the injustice and cruelty of life... Religion will not work automatically, however; it requires a great deal of effort and cannot succeed if it is facile, false, idolatrous or self-indulgent.' (2009: 305)

R. S. Thomas was clearly not under any illusion that talking about God is easy. Nor is it easy to talk about the central mystery of the Christian faith: the death and resurrection of Jesus. In fact, in confronting that event, the reason is torn. But if religion is not about providing answers, but enabling us to live creatively with the questions, then R. S. Thomas has indeed offered us true religion.

Thomas's volume *Counterpoint* was published in 1990 by Bloodaxe Books, the publishers of his last books of poetry. The poems in *Counterpoint* do not have individual titles but fall into four groups: BC, Incarnation, Crucifixion, AD. The cover illustration is of Vermeer's *A Lady Weighing Gold* which shows an attractive woman delicately holding up a pair of balances to see if they are true; and in the background is a painting of the Last Judgement. The whole book is an exercise in holding things in balance.

This is not an easy book, either in terms of understanding or in terms of the challenging concepts and language about God. There are echoes of the explosive language of *H'm*, with a God who seems distant and hostile:

God smiled. The controls
were working: the small
eaten by the large, the large
by the larger. One problem
remained: the immunity
of a species. 'Easy,'
the jester at his side
whispered, indicating
the air's window that the germs
thronged. God opened it
a crack, and the human edifice
was dismantled. (1990a: 19)

But this is a book of counterpoint, with one line of music playing against another, one idea bouncing off the other; the individual poems have to be held in tension with each other. On one side of the page, we read this:

Today
there is only this one option
before me. Remembering,
as one goes out into space,
on the way to the sun,
how dark it will grow,
I stare up into the darkness
of his countenance, knowing it
a reflection of the three days and nights
at the back of love's looking-
glass even a god must spend. (1990a: 36)

Leslie Griffiths gave an insightful address entitled *The Far Side of the Cross, the spirituality of R. S. Thomas* at the Methodist Conference in 1996. Griffiths picks up on Thomas's mirror imagery, a motif that runs through so much of his poetry, and explores this in conjunction with the Cross:

As the sun's light is reflected by the moon, so too God's love is reflected by the Cross. And just as the furies are at home in mirrors which reflect the strutting and fretting of sinful human beings, so too the cruelty and barbarity of the Cross are a reflection of those "tears at the heart of things" referred to by the Latin poet Virgil. So contemplation of the Cross can fill us with a sense of the enormity of God's love and also the depth of human sin. But beyond such thoughts lies the awesome mystery of God's own being. For the Cross is not simply a matter of what we see reflected either of God's love or our own wickedness. Behind it, at its far side, in the stillness, absence, silence, darkness, under the cloud of our unknowing, is the realm of ultimate and boundless mystery. (1996: 8)

This is not a God who is distant, in the sense of uncaring, but a God who has suffered for us in a way we cannot comprehend. This provides a different sort of distance, one of unknowing.

There is no group of poems in *Counterpoint* entitled 'resurrection'. But on the opposite page to the poem above we read the following:

Not the empty tomb
but the uninhabited
cross. Look long enough
and you will see the arms
put on leaves. Not a crown
of thorns, but a crown of flowers
haloing it, with a bird singing
as though perched on paradise's threshold. (1990a: 37)

However, to get such a vision of the transformation of the cross into a living tree, thorns into flowers, and the bird's music hinting of paradise, is not the transformation of a moment. It takes time. Waiting, that watchword of Thomas's:

I waited upon
him as a mirror
in its anonymity
waits upon absence.

Time passed. Once
from the closeness
of the invisible,
or in the after-draught

of the far-off, hurrying
about the immensity
of his being, I rose brimming
towards him like the spring-tide. (1990a: 45)

There is always the tension in R. S. Thomas of both being committed
to words, for words are how we make poetry, but being aware also that
a certain type of silence speaks louder than words. Thomas recognizes
that the psalmist was aware of this silent communication, too deep for
words. He makes explicit reference to Psalm 42, where the tortured
soul yearning for God in the way that the parched deer longs for cooling
streams, knows of the 'deep calling to deep':

But the silence in the mind
is when we live best, within
listening distance of the silence
we call God. This is the deep
calling to deep of the psalm-
writer, the bottomless ocean
we launch the armada of
our thoughts on, never arriving. (1990a: 50)

'Never arriving'. There is a recognition that although we are on a
journey and we have destinations in view, the provisionality of this life
means that we can never finally arrive at conceptions of God. This is
not failure, but a proper realization of our limitations as the created, not
the creator. But a communication of a sort ensues when we continue to
launch those exploratory thoughts, when there is a yearning for God and
for meaning.

With the Psalms still in mind, R. S. Thomas writes a matching poem
on the other side of the page: 'Were they so wrong who thought, when
/ it thundered, you were in a rage?' (1990a: 51, cf. Psalm 18). Protest,
outcry, rage before God was the response of the psalmists when they,

like Job, found themselves in the midst of suffering. This ability, this freedom we have been given to voice such protest, is what makes God God, suggests Thomas: 'What makes you God but the freedom / / you have given us to bellow our defiance / at you over the grave's maw' (1990a: 51, cf. Psalm 38).

The recognition that the journey might be a difficult one is not an excuse for refusing to set out. In fact we are almost impelled to do so, for we are like migratory birds pulled by our internal compass in a God-ward direction:

> He is that great void
> we must enter, calling
> to one another on our way
> in the direction from which
> he blows. What matter
> if we should never arrive
> to breed or to winter
> in the climate of our conception?
>
> Enough we have been given wings
> and a needle in the mind
> to respond to his bleak north.
>
> There are times even at the Pole
> when he, too, pauses in his withdrawal
> so that it is light there all night long. (1990a: 54)

'It is light there all night long'. We see again Thomas's ability to marry crucifixion and resurrection imagery, without the one supplanting the other. There is light to lighten our darkness. Or is it that the shadow (shadow of the cross?) that gives comfort? 'And to enthral the journey / that has no ending, once in a while / the falling of his shadow' (1990a: 59).

The final poem of this book is one of extreme simplicity. It is not arrival that is the goal, but being a little nearer, and knowing that is enough:

> I think that maybe
> I will be a little surer
> of being a little nearer.

That's all. Eternity
is in the understanding
that that little is more than enough. (1990a: 63)

In 1991 R. S. Thomas's wife Elsi died. His next book *Mass for Hard Times* (1992) was dedicated to her memory. The cross is present as ever, for by this time we realize that he comes back again and again, almost obsessively, to that point. In further elaboration of the concept of the reverse of the cross/mirror that we met in *Counterpoint*, he says 'Blessed be the far side of the Cross and the back / of the mirror, that they are concealed from us' (1992, 'Benedictus': 14).

When Leslie Griffiths read those words, he said 'I was instantly hooked by these images that have played with me ever since, drawing me, hauling me, flapping and thrashing, on to the shore of a dark and deep mystery' (1996: 5). This is what good poetry does. It invites, involves and takes time to reveal its secrets. To read Thomas's poetry of crucifixion and resurrection is to be involved in that rhythm that played so powerfully two thousand years ago in a unique way, but is always present. There is also however an understanding that is hidden from us – and for that we should be grateful.

When we speak of the cross it is often allied to repentance but what is repentance? This is not a word used much by R. S. Thomas, but this is not to say that what is behind that word is not frequently part of his thinking. For repentance is not simply being sorry, although that is part of it, but to repent is to see the world new, to turn round, to have a different orientation. It requires imagination to envisage things differently and here the poet helps us.

Perhaps we think repentance is something solely under our control, but Thomas, in the following words, suggests that it is something that happens to us, unexpectedly, and that it is linked with cross, and that the crucified body is the lightning conductor. As lightning strikes suddenly, unpredictably, the thoughts that are demolished come tumbling down not because we have chosen that it should be so, in time carefully set aside for such activity, but because they are obliterated by something from outside ourselves:

I count over the hours put by
for repentance, pulling thought's buildings
down to make way for the new,
fooling myself with the assurance

that when he occurs it is as the weather
of prayer's forecast, never with all
the unexpectedness of his body's
lightning, naked upon a cross. (1992, 'Retired': 23)

There are times when God can come in. The poem 'Match my
Moments' (1992: 44) tells of such occasions. The last two stanzas reflect
crucifixion and resurrection:

That time
the queue winding towards
the gas chambers, and the nun,
who had already died
to this world, to the girl
in tears: Don't cry. Look,
I will take your place.

That time
after the night's frost the tree
weeping, the miser in me
complaining: Why all this washing
the earth's feet in gold? And I,
my finger at my lips: Because
it is what we are made of.

The nun's death is a substitutionary one. But since she has already
died, so to speak, death has no dominion over her and therefore she can
live and die without fear of the evil spirit abroad in that place. The last
stanza has in the background an experience R. S. Thomas had at Manafon.
He tells about it in 'Former Paths' (*Autobiographies*, 1997a: 15):

There was a large ash tree at the entrance to the rectory lane that
would be completely yellow by November. One autumn the leaves
remained on it longer than usual. But there came a great frost one
night, and the following day, as the sun rose, the leaves began
to fall. They continued to fall for hours until the tree was like a
golden fountain playing silently in the sun; I shall never forget it.

The deciduous tree 'dies' as it sheds its leaves in a glorious fountain. In both these stanzas there are tears, weeping. But the tree will come to life again and there is glory, hushed reverence, in the air as leaves fall. This is a dying, but at the same time it is a glorious resurrection of the spirit, as it is with the nun who offered to die in the place of the other.

'And how contemporary / is the Cross, that long-bow drawn / against love?' R. S. Thomas asks in his 'Mass for Hard Times' (1992: 13). He further meditates on this in a short poem called, surprisingly, 'Sure', for the one thing we thought we could be sure about with R. S. Thomas is that he is not sure. Is the title going to be ironic?

Where the lamb died
a bird sings.
Where a soul perishes
What music? The cross

is an old-fashioned
weapon, but its bow
is drawn unerringly
against the heart. (1992: 53)

Being a rector of a rural parish R. S. Thomas was aware of the harsh realities of the farming life. He reports 'If a lamb died, there was nothing for it but to fling it into the hedge for the crows to eat their fill of it. Religion was a matter for Sundays' ('Former Paths' in *Autobiographies*, 1997a: 12). In this context, the singing bird seems somewhat sinister, but the death of a lamb does give life to another. Does the perishing soul have any answering redemptive music? The interjection of the cross suggests that this is to be some sort of answer. It may be old fashioned, but it is still relevant to our living, and our dying.

The cross transforms into a weapon in the hand of the archer and is effective as ever in reaching its target: its aim is sure and penetrates our hearts. But it could also be the bow in the hand of the stringed instrument player and be drawn against the heart to bring out the music. And we remember also the poem about Kreisler, in which the musician suffered himself on his instrument. Love dies on the cross, but it is simultaneously the way to pierce our hearts with redemptive music.

Although R. S. Thomas recognized that the appeal the cross ultimately makes is to the heart, he never abandoned his quest to understand with the mind. This took him so far, but it could not make the final connection:

There was something I was near
and never attained: a pattern,
an explanation. (1992, 'Sonata in X': 82)

It is the fish that got away:

Let me tell you that without
catching a thing I was not far
from the truth that time, since meaning
is not in having but trying.
Questioned, the trout had confessed
I was indistinguishable
from a tree, roots in darkness
my head in the clouds, and that
like thoughts, too, their best place
was among the shadows rather
than being drawn into the light's
dryness to perish of too much air. (1992, 'Afon Rhiw': 79)

Perhaps this is the problem with atonement theories, which take the metaphors of the Bible and try to explain how the crucifixion works. The fully worked-out thoughts do not leave enough room for the imagination; they cut off alternative lines of interpretation, so the thoughts begin to dry out, lose their vitality, from exposure to too much air.

Then comes the final book of his poetry published during his lifetime, aptly entitled *No Truce with the Furies* (1995). When R. S. Thomas started out as a young curate and then rector, it was the suffering he met on an individual basis as he ministered to his parishioners that prompted him to delve deeply into the problem of pain. He was shocked out of his comfortable orientation. His early life and his theological training had not equipped him to deal with the anguish he met on a regular, routine basis. He thought, he read, he pondered and prayed over his long life about these issues, and the cross becomes a focal point around which his reflections swirl.

As with the psalmist, and with Job, and even with Christ, lament and protest are an intrinsic part of such reflection. It is a disorienting experience to enter into the problem of suffering. Yet somehow the acknowledgement of the ordinary pain that is part of life brings a relief to the reader. Thomas's astringent take is actually cleansing and healing.

His refusal to let God off the hook also has a long biblical history in the protests of the voices of counter-testimony.

But there is also in Thomas a less fully acknowledged and recognized movement to hope. This is not a facile and easily voiced hope, for he has been through the mill and knows that easy optimism is not an option. Being a parish priest has kept him rooted in reality. Whatever conclusions he comes to has to be true for life as it is lived. As he started his ministry in visiting the sick and elderly, he is still visiting and this time it is an old peoples' home:

> What god is proud
> of this garden
> of dead flowers, this underwater
> grotto of humanity,
> where limbs wave in invisible
> currents, faces drooping
> on dry stalks, voices clawing
> in a last desperate effort
> to retain hold? ...
> Is this
> the best Rabbi Ben Ezra
> promised? I come away
> comforting myself, as I can,
> that there is another
> garden, all dew and fragrance,
> and that these are the brambles
> about it we are caught in,
> a sacrifice prepared
> by a torn god to a love fiercer
> than we can understand. (1995a, 'Geriatric': 9)

He comforts himself, as he can because of his confidence in the resurrection, as much as he can, because of his doubts, that there are better things to come. Love is at the heart of it, but it is a fierce love, one we struggle to understand. In what sense are our sufferings a sacrifice? There is no explanation, only the knowledge that, though we may be torn, the god is torn also.

If life in this world is a balance between pain and joy, on which side of the scales does the heavier weight fall? But the balances do not work in this mechanical way, they defy reason:

> But against
> all this I have seen the lamb
> gambolling for a moment, as though
> life were a good thing. This, I have said,
> is God's roguery, juggling
> with the scales, weighting the one
> pan down with evil piled
> upon evil then sending it suddenly
> sky-high with in the other a tear
> fallen from the hardest of eyes. (1995a, 'Mischief: 45)

There is crucifixion and there is resurrection and it would seem that the pain outweighs any compensation. But that is not how it works in God's world. It is a tear, the lightest drop, falling from the eye of someone, however hard hearted, who has succumbed to a resurrection experience – this is what sends the balance flying and gives the assurance that life is a good thing.

As he comes near the end of his personal journey (he died in 2000) R. S. Thomas wrote the poem 'At the End' (1995a: 42). A final explanation may have eluded him, he is still aware of the suffering in the world, but has his faith given him any way to live creatively in this world, whilst still holding those questions? This is what religion is for, suggests Karen Armstrong. Not to find answers, information, but to find some peace in the turmoil:

> Few possessions: a chair,
> a table, a bed
> to say my prayers by,
> and, gathered from the shore,
> the bone-like, crossed sticks
> proving that nature
> acknowledges the Crucifixion.
> At night I am at
> a window not too small
> to be frame to the stars
> that are no further off
> than the city lights
> I have rejected. By day

the passers-by, who are not
pilgrims, stare through the rain's
bars, seeing me as prisoner
of the one view, I who
have been made free
by the tide's pendulum truth
that the heart that is low now
will be at the full tomorrow.

As he reviews the resources he has at the end of his life and looks at
his few possessions, each has a significance. The driftwood sticks, in
the shape of the cross, provide acknowledgement that nature too knows
all about crucifixion. The beauty and the cruelty in nature has been a
constant theme in his poetry, for suffering is not simply a human issue
but belongs to the natural world also. His bed is not primarily there for
sleeping (he was an insomniac!) but a reminder of prayer that has been a
constant way of life for R. S. Thomas.

For a man who found the presence of God elusive, nevertheless
Thomas had a tenacity of spirit such that he never gave up praying,
waiting – not to control God but to be ready for the moment. His life had
also been one of eschewing the city lights. He found a resurrection of
the spirit in nature and could not have imagined living in a city. Being a
rural priest also gave him time, time to think and write poetry. But there
was still a price to pay as he poignantly expressed in a letter to his friend
Raymond Garlick:

I was glad to get your letter, too. It is socially very lonely here.
I don't suffer from loneliness, as I am always content to be alone
in nature like the Celtic saints. But complete mental conformism
in all one's neighbours can produce another kind of loneliness.
(2009: 77)

There is an allusive acknowledgement that he is a pilgrim, he has
been on a spiritual journey. And although those who are not similarly
pilgrims will not understand, he is not in fact a prisoner but a free man.
What understanding is it that has given him this freedom? The answer
lies in those last lines – he has 'been made free / by the tide's pendulum
truth / that the heart that is low now / will be at full tomorrow.'

The sea was important for R. S. Thomas. When he was absent from
its shores, he longed for that physical presence. Perhaps it was not only

the memory of his Anglesey childhood but the genetic inheritance from his sailor father. Sea imagery informed much of his writing and could speak of the depths of questioning and doubts he had to traverse in his walk with God.

But there is also another allusion that is present in those lines. In 1961 Thomas edited a book of poetry for children *The Batsford Book of Country Verse*. His selection was based on the poems he had loved as a boy. He explains: '[I]t was by way of nature that I myself came to poetry. I loved some of these poems because they expressed for me something of the environment in which I was brought up, the power and beauty of the sea, and the excitement and changeableness of the seasons' (1961b: 7). And one of those poems is an excerpt from Matthew Arnold's 'Dover Beach'.

The excerpt only includes the first stanza where we hear the rhythm of the waves that bring 'The eternal note of sadness in'. But famously, of course, for Arnold the 'Sea of Faith' was in withdrawal. There are times too when it seemed that was how it felt for R. S. Thomas but he came through to a time where the rhythm of the tide reflected his faith and his heart. In an earlier poem in *Laboratories of the Spirit* Thomas describes his experience of 'Sea-Watching' (1975: 64):

Grey waters, vast
    as an area of prayer
that one enters. Daily
    over a period of years
I have let my eye rest on them.
Was I waiting for something?
                        Nothing
but that continuous waving
    that is without meaning
occurred.
    Ah, but a rare bird is
rare. It is when one is not looking,
at times one is not there
               that it comes.
You must wear your eyes out,
as others their knees.

There was no sense that prayer, religion, the experience of God was an easy thing, obtained without effort and dedication. But the 'rare bird' did come to him in the end and gave him the understanding that the sea of faith was not in permanent withdrawal, the tide would turn.

In this book I have been suggesting that R. S. Thomas's engagement with the perplexities of life and faith has followed a dynamic of disorientation and new orientation, and that this is an echo of that rhythm of crucifixion and resurrection. As he reaches the end of his life there is a confidence that the heart will be at full tomorrow. But the title, 'At the end', perhaps is suggestive that in the end, when all things are done, not only when the individual life on this earth is over, but at the end of all things, the *eschaton*, the rhythm will culminate in a fullness, in resurrection, the true Resurrection from which all our lesser resurrections derive.

The biblical Job came to the conclusion that although there were many things he did not know nevertheless, as a result of the experience of God communicating with him, he could reject, 'repent', of the assessment of himself as no more than dust and ashes. R. S. Thomas similarly concludes, in an earlier poem, that we are not destined for dust:

> I will not
> be here long, but have seen
> (among people) distorted
> bodies, haloed with love,
> shedding a radiance
> where flies hung smaller
> than the dust they say
> man came from and to which,
> I say, he will not return. (1986, 'The Fly': 8)

'Dust you are, to dust you will return', the Lord God said to the first humans, following the disobedient eating from the forbidden tree (Genesis 3: 19). R. S. Thomas would have taken many funeral services in his time as a priest and repeated the words 'earth to earth, ashes to ashes, dust to dust'. But the destiny of humanity set forth in Genesis is transformed by the preceding words of that service for it says; 'in sure and certain hope of the resurrection to eternal life though our Lord Jesus Christ'. Resurrection provides a greater hope than our biological destiny would suggest.

But R. S. Thomas would not be the Thomas we have got to know, if we left things so tidily resolved. The word 'resurrection' has been sparely used by Thomas, even if the concept is far more evident than

absence of the word suggests. He did however write a poem entitled
'Resurrections' (1995a: 47), but it is subversive as ever:

Easier for them, God
only at the beginning
of his recession...
                    What
happened? Suddenly he was
gone, leaving love guttering
in his withdrawal. And scenting
disaster, as flies are attracted
to a carcase, far down
in the subconscious the ghouls
and the demons we thought
we had buried for ever resurrected.

It is a warning against trying to be too tidy, to assume there is a neat
resolution to his poetry. R. S. Thomas is the voice of counter-testimony
and he will never, if read as a whole, make for easy comfortable listening.
We must not try to tame him.

Afterword

As part of the BBC Poetry Season in the summer of 2009, Armando Iannucci explored his passion for the poetry of John Milton (2009). During the course of this TV programme he said that he had once been asked, on air, why he had given up his (very early) thoughts of becoming a priest. Part of the reason, he said, was that in all his theological explorations no one had ever explained to him why Jesus had to die to save humankind. He heard the assertion again and again, but never heard an explanation.

Iannucci anticipated that this confession would bring him a large postbag; and he was not wrong. He kept those many communications and held them in his hand as he talked to us. They were well meaning and ranged from the short and pithy to the long and detailed. He read us some excerpts. But as he put to one side the sheaf of papers with something of a sigh, it was obvious that none of these explanations satisfied him. His conclusion was – don't ask the question.

But what if there is a different way of doing theology? Not in refusing to ask the questions, but framing the consequent thoughts not as concise theoretical explanations, but in poetry? Can this not in fact meet a deep need, in the exploration of God, in the language about God, not in terms of answers, but enabling people to live the questions appropriately and imaginatively?

As I suggested in chapter one, theory is not enough. Our scientific age has seduced us into thinking that we can give scientific answers to life's big questions. R. S. Thomas addressed this:

> We are told with increasing vehemence that this is a scientific age, and that science is transforming the world, but is it not also a mechanized and impersonal age, an analytic and clinical one; an age in which under the hard gloss of affluence there can be detected the murmuring of the starved heart and the uneasy spirit? "The voice of Rachel crying for her children, and would not be comforted, because they are not." ... Perhaps it is the attempt of contemporary Christianity to be reasonable in the face of science that makes it so innocuous. It is certainly our increasing isolation from Geoffrey Hill's "common, puddled substance" that makes us less and less capable of statements like "a deep distress hath humanised my soul", and so less and less capable of sustaining that

creative tension of the intellect and the emotions out of which the good life and the good poem can be born. ('A Frame for Poetry' in *Selected Pro*se, 1995b: 72,73)

The tension between the intellect and emotions, the mind or reason and the heart, has been a consistent feature of R. S. Thomas's poetry. It is not that the mind is abandoned, that anything goes, but that it finally is not enough. William Blake's assertion was that the contraries of reason and heart needed to be held in tension. In the posthumously published collection of R. S. Thomas's poetry, entitled *Residues*, there is a poem about the essential features of poetry. It starts, 'Don't ask me; / I have no recipe / for a poem.' – Thomas was always wary of giving any theoretical construction for the making of a poem. But it concludes

Ask no rhyme
of a poem, only
that it keep faith

with life's rhythm.
Language will trick
you if it can.
Syntax is words'

way of shackling
the spirit. Poetry is that
which arrives at the intellect
by way of the heart. (2002: 69)

This is how the two are held together, the heart and the intellect. The heart does actually have a knowledge that is intellectually sound, and poetry comes to birth by that route. Note also that it must be true to life's rhythm. This is where R. S. Thomas started out on his poetic pilgrimage of his adult years, when he saw real life and realized that it undermined his theoretical, protected, understanding and he entered into an experience of disorientation that lasted, on and off, for the rest of his life.

The psalmist and Job speak of disorientation and this experience was necessary for their simplistic ideas of God to be challenged. Did Christ also go through disorientation as he withdrew to the wilderness and as he agonized in the garden? There is always the danger of idolatry, worshipping a false god, and the way of disorientation can dismantle the false god.

But what of those who are comfortable in the old orientation? R. S. Thomas considers this in the poem 'The Valley Dweller' (1977: 10):

> He heard that there were other places
> but he never saw them. No travellers
> came back to him with gold on their boots,
> with sand even. What was his life
> worth? Was there a tree he did not eat
> of, because he was not tempted
> to? And must we praise him for it?
>
> I have visited his valley:
> beautiful enough, the trees' braziers
> alight, the clouds tall, the river,
> coming from somewhere far off, hurrying
> where? Is wisdom refraining
> from thinking about it? And is there
> the one question we must not put?
>
> He looked in this mirror, saw that
> for all its wateriness his image
> was not erased; listened while
> life lasted to what it seemed
> to be saying to him between
> two sides of a valley, which
> was not much, but sufficient for him.

For some the familiar contours are enough. R. S. Thomas does not say that the valley dweller should get out more. But for some, the sides of the valley are not a comforting, familiar, safe place but the sides of a prison. R. S. Thomas was always striding (both literally and metaphorically) across the high, sometimes bleak, moors and mountains. The voices of counter-testimony cannot live comfortably, permanently, in the valley.

There are surely people who need to hear (perhaps now more than ever?) the voices of counter-testimony in the pursuit of truth. This is not to dismantle faith, but to sustain it when theological constructions are challenged by life as it is lived. Barry Morgan says: 'At various moments of crisis in my own ministry it was to his poetry I turned for both illumination and sustenance since he was never satisfied with glib, easy answers to complicated questions of faith' (2006: 8).

Central to R. S. Thomas's explorations is the cross of Christ. After reading his poetry do we now understand the cross? That is not the point, for we are invited with him into the disorientation of the cross, the mystery of that event, the scandal of Christ's suffering and rejection. Thomas gives us then the freedom (which we would already have had if we have been listening to the biblical voices of counter-testimony) to explore for ourselves, to look at it from different angles; but not to ignore it for we must take it seriously. McGill concludes:

> For Thomas the question remained the Cross itself. Yet, if he was uneasy with the story, he was no less uneasy with the trivialization of it in our own times, the ready de-mythologizing, the rationalistic posturings, the peculiar assumption that somehow the discoveries of the vastness of the universe have diminished God. Perhaps, perhaps after all, the Cross must not mean, but simply be. (2004: 192)

R. S. Thomas wrote out of his experience and the reflection on that experience. In translating those thoughts into poetry for us, the intention is not that we simply inhabit the same territory as Thomas but that we take that gift and use it for our own imaginings, as a stimulus to our own appropriation of that event. As Thomas writes:

> I must choose words and rhythms which will keep it fresh and have the power to recreate the experience in all its original intensity for each new reader. But in this very process the experience is changed, and will continue to be changed as each new reader apprehends it. (1995b: 65)

Thomas, in his introduction to the Psalms, said that they were 'the expression of a nation's sorrow and exultation in the search for God' and that in them we can find 'our feelings eloquently expressed for us in our own attempts to find God and glorify him' (1997b: 7). The dynamic of sorrow and exultation and the eloquent expression of our feelings is present for us also in R. S. Thomas's poetry.

It is often acknowledged that he is a poet of the cross, but it is less frequently recognized that Thomas is a poet of resurrection too. His language of resurrection may be more suggestive and less direct than the language of the cross, but the intention is to bring us to the point where we find, or are found by, God, see the world differently as a result, and can indeed give glory to him. But as with the psalmist, that movement from lament to praise comes as a mixture of strenuous searching and pure gift. Thomas explains it as follows:

> And without warning and without effort a little poem formed in my mind... And certainly, as with a poem, it is thus that He sometimes chooses to come. But also, just as a poem sometimes comes after a very long period of thinking and searching, doesn't God come in the same way after a long period on your knees, or of reading and studying? And yet it cannot be proved and demonstrated. It isn't the result of long and refined reasoning, but communication that is at once mysterious and direct. (*Autobiographies*, 1997a: 165,166)

But does poetry change us, for salvation, atonement, is about learning how to be good again in relationship with God in Christ? Brueggemann suggests that it does. 'If we wish to have transformed obedience (i.e., more faithful, responsive listening), then we must be summoned to an alternative imagination, in order that we may imagine the world and ourselves differently... It is poetic invitation that holds the only chance of changed behavior' (1989: 85).

R. S. Thomas's poetry of crucifixion and resurrection takes us into territory beyond the theoretical, rational explanations of the event. Our imaginations are challenged, stretched and invigorated. Sometimes we are shocked, but the biblical witness to the voices of counter-testimony show that language about and to God is sometimes shocking as we wrestle with the perplexities of life and the mystery of God. But then Thomas will suddenly disarm us with words of tenderness, vision and utter breathtaking beauty that turn us around to see things quite differently in the newness of the resurrection morning.

There are many things we still do not understand. But the poet can leave things ragged, torn, and be suggestive rather than producing proofs. Perhaps this facility is the one most suited to the exploration of crucifixion and resurrection.

Bibliography

Works by R. S. Thomas

Poetry
(1955) *Song at the Year's Turning*, London: Rupert Hart-Davis
(1958) *Poetry for Supper*, London: Rupert Hart-Davis
(1961a) *Tares*, London: Rupert Hart-Davis
(1963a) *The Bread of Truth*, London: Rupert Hart-Davis
(1966) *Pietá*, London: Rupert Hart-Davis
(1968) *Not that he Brought Flowers*: Rupert Hart-Davis
(1972a) *H'm*, London: Macmillan
(1975) *Laboratories of the Spirit*, London: Macmillan
(1977) *The Way Of It*, South Shields: Ceolfrith Press
(1978) *Frequencies*, London: Macmillan
(1981) *Between Here and Now*, London: Macmillan
(1983a) *Later Poems 1972-1983*, London: Macmillan
(1985) *Destinations*, Shipston-on-Stour: The Celandine Press
(1986) *Experimenting with an Amen*, London: Macmillan
(1988) *The Echoes Return Slow*, London: Macmillan
(1990a) *Counterpoint*, Newcastle upon Tyne: Bloodaxe
(1992) *Mass for Hard Times*, Newcastle upon Tyne: Bloodaxe
(1995a) *No Truce with the Furies*, Newcastle upon Tyne: Bloodaxe
(2002) *Residues*, Tarset, Northumberland: Bloodaxe

(1993) *Collected Poems 1945-1990*, London: Phoenix
(2004) *Collected Later Poems 1988-2000*, Tarset: Bloodaxe
(2003) *R. S. Thomas, Selected Poems*, London: Penguin Group

Prose
(1995b) *R. S. Thomas, Selected Prose*, 3rd edition, ed Sandra Anstey,
   Bridgend: Seren Books
(1997a) *R. S. Thomas, Autobiographies*, translated from Welsh by Jason
   Walford Davies, London: Dent
(1997b) Foreword to *The Psalms: Ancient Poetry of the Spirit*, Oxford:
   Lion
(2009) *R. S. Thomas: Letters to Raymond Garlick 1951-1999*, ed
   J.W.Davies, Llandysul: Gomer

Books edited

(1961b) *The Batsford Book of Country Verse*, London: B.T.Batsford Ltd

(1963b) *The Penguin Book of Religious Verse*, Harmondsworth:
Penguin Books

(1967) *A Choice of George Herbert's Verse*, London: Faber and Faber

Other sources of R. S. Thomas texts

(1972b) 'R. S. Thomas, Priest and Poet. Transcript of BBC TV
programme. Produced by John Ormond', *Poetry Wales*, Vol 7, No 4,
Spring, pp 47-57

(1983b) *'R. S. Thomas talks to J.B.Lethbridge'*, Anglo-Welsh Review,
Vol 74, pp 35-56

(1990b) 'Probings: An interview with R. S. Thomas', *Planet 80*, pp 28-52

(2001) 'R. S. Thomas in Conversation with Molly Price-Owen, *The
David Jones Journal*, R. S. Thomas Special Issue, Summer/Autumn
2001, pp 93-102

Recordings

(1991) *The South Bank Show*, ITV, Broadcast 17 February 1991

(1999) *R. S. Thomas Reading the Poems*, triple CD, producer Damian
Walford Davies; Sain Records C2209

Other works

Alison, J. (2003) *On Being Liked*, London: Darton, Longman & Todd

Armstrong, K. (2005) *The Spiral Staircase*, London: Harper Perrenial

Armstrong, K. (2009) *The Case for God*, London: The Bodley Head

Avis, P. (1999) *God and the Creative Imagination*, London: Routledge

Baal-Teshuva, J. (2008) *Chagall*, Los Angeles: Taschen

Barr, J. (1992*) The Garden of Eden and the Hope of Immortality*,
London: SCM Press

Barth, J.R. (2001) *The Symbolic Imagination, Coleridge and the
Romantic Tradition*, NewYork: Fordham University Press

Bielenberg, C. (1984) *The Past is Myself*, London: Corgi Books

Brueggemann, W. (1984*) The Message of the Psalms*, Minneapolis:
Augsburg Publishing House

Brueggemann, W. (1989) *Finally Comes the Poet*, Minneapolis:
Fortress Press

Brueggemann, W. (1997) *Theology of the Old Testament*, Minneapolis:
Fortress Press

Brueggemann, W. (1999) *Deep Memory Exuberant Hope*, Minneapolis: Fortress Press

Burridge, R. A. (2007) *Imitating Jesus*, Michigan: Wm. B. Eerdmans

Caird, G.B. (1980*) The Language and Imagery of the Bible*, London: Gerald Duckworth & Co Ltd

Catchpole, D. (2006) *Jesus People, The Historical Jesus and the Beginnings of Community*, London: Darton, Longman & Todd

Chevalier, T. (2007) *Burning Bright*, London: HarperCollins

Cornish, J. (2002) *First Light*, London: Aurum Press

Davies, D.W. (ed)(2003) *Echoes to the Amen*, Cardiff: University of Wales Press

Davis, W.V. (2007) *R. S. Thomas, Poetry and Theology*, Waco: Baylor University Press

Driver, J. (2005) *Understanding the Atonement for the Mission of the Church*, Eugene Origon: Wipf & Stock

Dyson, A.E. (ed.) (1990) *Three Contemporary Poets, Thom Gunn, Ted Hughes and R. S. Thomas*, Basingstoke: Macmillan Education

Fiddes, P.S. (1989) *Past Event and Present Salvation*, London: Darton, Longman & Todd

Good, E.M. (1990) *In Turns of Tempest: A Reading of Job with Translation*, Stanford: Stanford University Press

Green, J.B. & Baker, M.D. (2000) *Recovering the Scandal of the Cross*, Illinois: IVP Academic

Griffiths, L.J. (1996*) The Far Side of the Cross, The Spirituality of R. S. Thomas*, Exeter: The Methodist Sacramental Fellowship

Harries, R. (2001) 'The Via Negativa in the Poetry of R. S. Thomas', *The David Jones Journal*, R. S. Thomas Special Issue, Summer/ Autumn 2001, pp 59-73

Hopewell, J.F. (1987) *Congregation: Stories and Structures*, Philadelphia: Fortress Press

Hosseini, K. (2003) *The Kite Runner*, London: Bloomsbury Publishing Plc

Iannucci, A. (2009*) Milton's Heaven and Hell*, Broadcast on 28 May 2009, BBC2

Lethbridge,L. & O'Grady,S. (eds.) (2002) *A Deep but Dazzling Darkness*, London: Darton, Longman & Todd

Matterson, S. & Jones, D. (2000) *Studying Poetry*, London: Hodder Arnold

McFague, S. (1982) *Metaphorical Theology*, Phildadelphia: Fortress Press

McGill, W.J. (2004) *Poets' Meeting: George Herbert, R. S. Thomas and the Argument with God*, Jefferson, North Carolina: McFarland & Co

Middleton, C. (2006) 'The Road to Romance', *Radio Times*, February, p. 14

Morgan, B. (2006*) Strangely Orthodox*, Llandysul: Gomer Press

Obama, B. (2007*) Dreams from my Father*, Edinburgh: Canongate Books Ltd

Phillips, D.Z. (1986) *R. S. Thomas, Poet of the Hidden God*, Pennsylvania: Pickwick Publications

Pohier, J. (1985) *God in Fragments*, translated from French by John Bowden, London: SCM Press

Riddell, M., Pierson, M. & Kirkpatrick, C., (2000) *The Prodigal Project*, London: SPCK

Roberts, J. (2007*) William Blake's Poetry*, London: Continuum

Soskice, J.M. (1985) *Metaphor and Religious Language*, Oxford: Clarendon Press

Thomas, M.W. (ed) (1993) *The Page's Drift, R. S. Thomas at Eighty*, Bridgend: Seren Books

Ward, J.P. (1987) *The Poetry of R. S. Thomas*, Bridgend: Poetry Wales Press

Wheeler Robinson, H. (1955) *The Cross in the Old Testament*, London: SCM

Williams, H.A. (1965*) The True Wilderness*, London: Constable and Company Ltd

Williams, R. (1994) *Open to Judgement*, London: Darton, Longman & Todd

Williams, R. (2000) *Christ on Trial*, London: HarperCollins

Williams, R. (2002) *The Poems of Rowan Williams*, Grand Rapids: Eerdmans

Williams, R. (2003) Foreword to *be Glad: An Incredible String Band Compendium*, Ed Adrian Whittaker, London: Helter Skelter Publishing

Wright, A. (1972) *Blake's Job: A Commentary*, Oxford: Oxford University Press

Wynn, M.R. (2005) *Emotional Experience and Religious Understanding*, Cambridge: Cambridge University Press

Unless otherwise stated, biblical references are taken from the Revised English Bible.